Hereward College

LEARNING RESOURCES
CENTRE

ACCESS ALL AREAS

Behind the Scenes at Coronation Street

ACCESS ALL AREAS

Behind the Scenes at Coronation Street

Words by **David Hanson** *with* **Jo Kingston**
Photographs by **Roger Dixon**

GRANADA
MEDIA

Acknowledgements

Special thanks to everyone on the *Coronation Street* production team for their co-operation and help with this book, and to Glenda Young for her patience and invaluable word processing skills. Thanks also to Mum, Dad and Stephen for their encouragement.

Jo Kingston

I'd like to thank everyone involved with *Coronation Street* during my time here who have helped make the top job so enjoyable. Thanks also to my wife, Anne, and my children for their support and enthusiasm.

David Hanson

Coronation Street is based on an idea by Tony Warren

First published in Great Britain in 1999 by Granada Media

an imprint of André Deutsch Limited in association with Granada Media
76 Dean Street London W1V 5HA
www.vci.co.uk

Copyright © Granada Media Group 1999

The right of Jo Kingston to be identified as the author of this work has been asserted by her in accordance with the Copyright, Designs and Patents Act 1988

10 9 8 7 6 5 4 3 2 1

A catalogue record for this book is available from the British Library

ISBN 0 233 99722 9

Design by DW Design, London

Printed in Italy by Grafiche Editoriali Padane S.p.A.

Contents

Foreword by Roger Dixon

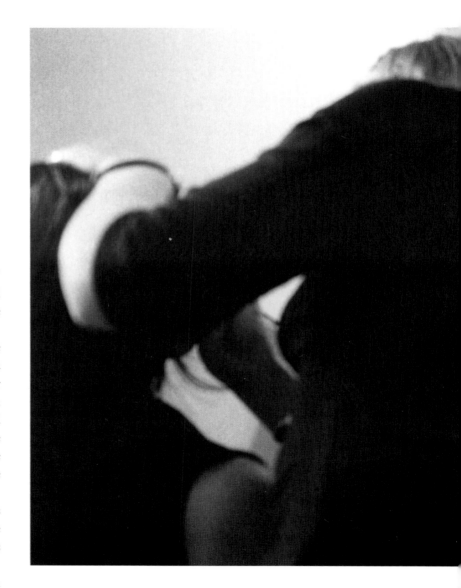

When I started this project I have to admit that I wasn't a 'natural' *Coronation Street* fan, but over the past months, working with all the different departments that go towards making the show, I have really grown to admire the *Street* and all its inhabitants.

I was both privileged and excited to be invited behind the scenes, but I can honestly say that I have never worked with such a dedicated and hardworking team – they really do work a 12-hour shift. From the biggest star of the moment, through the production team, the dressers, the make-up artists and the camera and sound crews, both in the studio and on location, I was staggered at the complex operation involved in bringing a single episode to the screen. It was fascinating to watch the 'birth' of a storyline and see it develop until it finally appears on the screen.

The wonderful thing for me was that I was allowed on this hallowed turf as an observer. None of the photographs you will see in this book have been specifically set up – they are all taken as documentary images.

There is such a wealth of material (I felt that I could have gone on finding new aspects to photograph for years) that the problem has been selecting which photographs to leave out. So as one (albeit new) *Coronation Street* fan to another, I hope you find that this book shows you a broader and different side of the *Street*.

Introduction

Producing *Coronation Street* is an overwhelming responsibility. With 18 million regular viewers and a 39-year history, it is a programme that touches other people's lives on a daily basis. Since the very first episode on 9 December 1960, *Corrie* has become a national institution. Everybody seems to have an opinion about the characters and stories. And as soon as I took over at the helm, all my friends and family suddenly became less interested in the details of my own life, and more interested in plying me with advice about the lives of Jack, Vera and Natalie.

It's a very demanding job, and on occasions you do feel the full glare of the nation's attention and expectations focused upon you. However, none of this can dissipate the joy of being in charge of a show like *Coronation Street*, and it is hugely rewarding. The first time I realised the weight of responsibility I was carrying was when I told my two eldest sons that I was to become the 27th producer of the *Street*. My eldest son immediately exclaimed, 'That's really great – you're going to be famous.' The other son didn't say anything for five full minutes, and then turned to me and said, 'Oh, Dad, don't cock it up.' That's real pressure!

Over the years there have been almost 5000 episodes of *Coronation Street*. Several of its actors and actresses, as well as its creator Tony Warren MBE, have received merits at the Palace, and it has been shown all over the world from Australia to Zambia. At its peak it pulled in a staggering 26.6 million viewers when Hilda Ogden left the programme on Christmas Day 1987, and its popularity has rarely wavered since.

When I took over *Coronation Street*, the show was again right at the top of the ratings. It was wonderful to inherit a show that was number one, but I believe it is my job to keep it there, and even improve on it. Any initial worries I had were partly allayed, though, because I already knew most of the cast, crew and writers, many of whom I had worked with on other shows, so there was a sense of history there.

I started work at Granada Television in 1979, and after three years as a script editor, I became a floor manager on the *Street*. In those days there were only two episodes a week, and we had few permanent sets. Most of the sets were put up and taken down as needed, so the cast rehearsed on the second floor beneath where my office is now. One of my earliest tasks was to mark up the floor of the rehearsal room.

Those were the days of Stan Ogden, Annie Walker and Albert Tatlock, and *Coronation Street* has changed a lot since then. Bill Podmore was the producer, and the *Street* was seen as a good training ground for staff. Although we only produced half the material we do now, it still seemed like a lot because it was the fastest programme we made at the time, and many other productions like *Brideshead Revisited* were taken at a very slow pace indeed.

Today the *Street* is even faster, as well as being more modern and having a much larger cast. It isn't that the programme was like a cottage industry in those days, but there was less pressure in terms of expectations. There was also less competition, with the only other soap opera being *Crossroads*. Now *Coronation Street* is a huge

Top: A studio floor plan showing where each of the *Street* sets are situated. **Bottom:** David Hanson (second from right) on the studio floor.

8

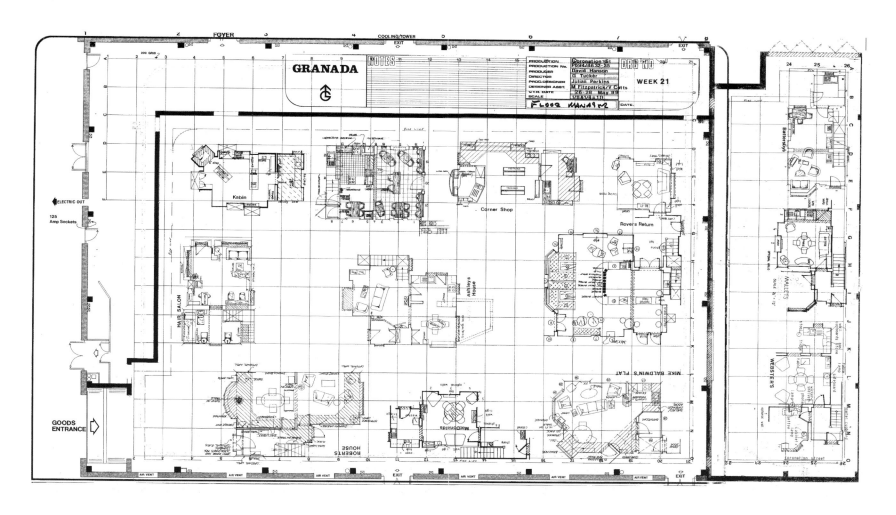

commercial enterprise and there is an enormous commitment to staying on top.

Of course the programme has moved on a lot since the early days – in terms of content as well as production methods. As audiences grow older you want to keep their loyalty but at the same time it's necessary to usher in a new generation, and *Coronation Street* has done that wonderfully over the years with an influx of young talent. There is always going to be some space at the younger end of the market, and I think we address that.

With so many fans around the world feeling that they have a personal stake in *Coronation Street*, it would be foolish not to take on board viewers' opinions. Obviously I can't read every single viewer's letter that comes in, but if there is a particularly strong complaint or exuberant praise then I like to see it.

From the constant feedback we receive, we are kept aware of which characters most capture the public imagination. At the moment Roy and Hayley are very popular, and Mike Baldwin remains so, despite all the tricks he's pulled over the years. The

Top: David Hanson attends a story conference.
Far left and bottom: Fascinated fans visit the *Street* set.

Battersbys divide opinion, but Rita and the Duckworths are loved right across the board and always have been. You can see where people are coming from. They like characters that play a lot of comedy, and characters that have a lot of history. But at the same time they are open to new characters, and our biggest audience in the last three years, reaching over 20 million, was for the wedding day of two relatively new characters that I had just brought in, Sharon Gaskell and Ian Bentley. That was very gratifying for me, because it showed we are still getting it right.

One of the best things about producing *Coronation Street* is having a wonderful team to work with. Everyone from the writers and actors to the entire crew are consummate professionals. The team carry on doing their jobs well no matter what, and that is why I think the majority of the *Street*'s audience will always stay loyal to it. If you keep producing quality then the fans will remain with you.

I like to be quite hands-on as a producer, although because the show goes out 52 weeks a year, the job is limited by time and it isn't possible to do absolutely everything. I do like to get involved in the minutiae, though, and on top of everything else there is to be done, I often find myself having the most ludicrous conversations about a character's hairstyle or the colour of their T-shirt.

In order to produce *Coronation Street* it is necessary to be a fan of the programme. You have to genuinely care about each and every character, and be aware of their histories. It is one of *Coronation Street*'s strengths that people do feel a great involvement with characters, having grown up with them and invested a lot of time in them, and there aren't many other programmes that can do that.

For many years now, what goes on behind the scenes on Britain's most famous street has been kept a closely guarded secret. But now we are prepared to open the doors and let the viewers in on it. From the first germ of an idea for a storyline to the last touches to the finished programme, this book gives you a guided tour around the creative processes of *Coronation Street* – and we hope you enjoy the trip.

1

From

Page *to*

Screen

Where Coronation Street begins

At the basis of a great drama serial there has to be great stories, believable characters and quality scripts. And *Coronation Street* has these in abundance, which is part of the reason that Weatherfield has remained so close to the hearts of the nation over the last 39 years.

But before these come to completion there is a long and detailed process to go through. If you wanted to build a house, you would employ an architect to draw up some plans rather than racing straight in to lay the bricks at random. And *Coronation Street* is conceived in exactly the same way. Before the writers get to work producing their scripts, many intensive hours are spent laying the foundations for plot and character, and coming up with a cohesive sequence of events for future episodes.

Every two weeks the creative process kicks off with a story conference, which takes place upstairs on the outdoor street set.

The bricks and mortar that viewers and visitors to Granada Studio Tours fondly imagine to front the bedrooms of the Mallets and McDonalds actually conceal a bright and modern conference room where the destinies of each and every *Coronation Street* character are decided around a huge square table. Here marriages are made and lives are lost, affairs are started and family feuds resolved. For an entire day, every *Corrie* character from Emily Bishop to Les Battersby is discussed and dissected by the producer, executive producer, script and story editors, story associates and writers – and what comes out of these conversations eventually decides what will

Writers and storyliners meet to discuss up-and-coming episodes.

be seen on screen months later. Over coffee, biscuits and mineral water, the team of men and women play with the lives of the nation's favourite folk like modern-day versions of the gods at Olympus.

Ever since Tony Warren penned the first six scripts that were to eventually become Britain's longest-running series, writing teams have come to *Coronation Street* at a fixed point. When a story conference begins there are already plots in motion and established characters, and because of this only certain options are possible. The team must take into account each of the characters, what kind

of people they are and what opportunities they have in life. They must be aware of what has gone before and of each character's likes, dislikes and limitations. Then, they must come up with ingenious and interesting stories, but most importantly, ones that work in conjunction with the characters.

The stories of *Coronation Street* are the universal stories of life on a small community scale. Love, hate, rivalry, greed, jealousy and crime all figure prominently, and long-term writer John Stevenson admits to drawing inspiration from pantomime, the Bible and Shakespeare as well as some of the more day-to-day aspects of his

own life. 'When Rita gave Sharon the Kabin it was the core of *King Lear*,' he explains. 'He gave his kingdom to his children and didn't like what they did with it, but it was too late. And any stories of irrational jealousy are *Othello*. Then again, Annie Walker's driving lessons came straight from my mum. She learned to drive in the 1960s and frightened the life out of various examiners. They eventually let her pass on the seventh attempt and I thought it would be just right for Annie Walker.'

Of course, if you were to minutely examine the history of *Coronation Street* it would become immediately obvious that those ordinary people in that little back street have had more eventful lives than the most outrageous Hollywood stars. Even a quiet character like Emily Bishop has had one husband murdered, another found to be a bigamist, suffered a nervous breakdown and been jilted by a vicar. And with 22 girlfriends, four children and three wives behind him, you can begin to see why Bill Roache is fond of calling his character Ken Barlow a 'one-man Greek tragedy'.

However, it is the way in which the stories are executed that makes them convincing to the viewer. And that is why attention to detail is so important – and why creating *Coronation Street* is such a painstaking process.

The story conferences usually begin quite peacefully. The story editor will come with an agenda of things that need to be discussed for the next eight episodes. There will be some stories already up and running that have to be picked up from the last block, and everyone will debate how they should continue from there. Usually there will be one very strong story that provides a spine for the rest, and several others of different magnitude and at different stages of completion.

Coronation Street always works from the character outwards. Each one has a distinct personality and reacts to situations in a unique way, and it is important not to make them interchangeable. If one episode ends with Emily discovering someone else's secret, she would have a huge dilemma about whether to reveal it, but if Audrey were the eavesdropper, then it would be implausible if she

didn't pass the gossip on straight away. Similarly, Mike Baldwin could conceivably start an affair with a colleague even while hoping for reconciliation with his estranged wife after being blackmailed over a previous adultery. Cautious Ken, on the other hand,

probably wouldn't make the same mistake twice – or at least not so soon afterwards!

By the end of the conference hopefully a consensus of opinion will have been reached among the writers, story associates and producer. However, it is inevitable that there are arguments from time to time. There are some very strong personalities around the writing table, and people can be proprietorial about their favourite characters. One person could suggest something and another might hotly contest that the character would never behave that way in a million years. These different viewpoints can result in huge rows, and it isn't unknown for people to storm out during a meeting.

Often the most volatile exchanges take place during the long-

Storyline conferences are the starting point for every scene which appears on television.

term story conference which happens every few months when the crop of current stories is reaching completion. Each and every character will be reviewed, and no punches are pulled. Some writers turn up with a very general idea, some with a more specific one, but nothing is ever set in stone. Although the long-term conference provides a good overview, storylines seized on at this stage may well twist and turn along the way, and can bear little resemblance to the original by the time they are finally screened.

Some writers are enthused by certain characters at a particular time, and everybody has their own perennial favourites. Occasionally a character won't have had any stories for a long while, and it will look as though they have run their natural course. Then at another conference someone might have a brilliant idea for a previously uninspiring person and they are granted a reprieve – for the time being.

After the bank of stories has been stocked up at the long-term conference, those ideas are fed into the fortnightly conferences at various points and examined in detail when the time is judged right to play them out. It's a slow, organic process, which ensures that by the time a story reaches the screen it has been discussed from all angles and thoroughly examined for plausibility and continuity.

When the story conference is over, the four story associates, under the guidance of the story editor, have the job of sitting down and organizing the ideas into structured episodes. Sometimes, if there hasn't been a unanimous decision in conference, it can be a nightmare, or 'like trying to juggle jelly,' as ex-story editor and current script writer David Lane puts it. The team untangle the ideas and fit them into the episodes in specific terms. So if, for example, Ashley was to propose to Maxine in the final episode of a block, they would work out how the story could be gradually led to that point over the next eight programmes.

Once the block is planned, each story associate takes away two episodes and has a few days to put flesh on the bones of the stories. It's a very specific process. An episode of *Coronation Street* usually has between 16 and 21 scenes and there are certain rules to remember. The production co-ordinator will have provided a list of available artists and the storyliners have to work around it. When a large amount of characters need to be fitted into an episode, the Rovers Return and Roy's Rolls are ideal vehicles for scenes. Daran Little provides archive information – whether it is someone's birthday or the anniversary of a character's death, and things such as school vacations and Bank Holidays are also taken into account.

So even if you do see Underworld open on a Bank Holiday Monday, you can bet Janice or Deirdre will mention the overtime or Baldwin's slave-driving.

Storyline documents set the mood and tone for each scene, while outlining where it is to be set and with which characters. It is also necessary at this stage to bear in mind how many scenes are to be shot in studio, how many on the street lot and how many at an outside location. An imbalance either way will make filming schedules impossible a few weeks further down the line.

After much discussion and review, the final drafts are then handed to me for approval the following Wednesday. On the Thursday we have a long storyline meeting where I give my input. I usually make one or two changes, and when they have been added the definitive five- or six-page documents are sent out to the commissioned writers.

Going through the list of available writers and trying to match them up to episodes is another responsibility of the producer. Some may have an interest in certain storylines or characters and ask to write a particular episode because they feel they can do it justice. Outstanding comedy writers may be given a high comedy episode, whereas others prefer big set-pieces like weddings and funerals.

Sometimes scenes may not look very funny or tragic when set out in a bald fashion, so it depends on the skill of the individual to develop the comedy or pathos in the script. Luckily, we have a great writing team on *Coronation Street* and they are always able to bring the plots convincingly to life.

However, writers are creative people, and don't always slavishly follow the storylines. Each likes to put his or her individual stamp on to an episode, and any comments and suggestions are discussed at a commissioning conference. These are usually held on a Tuesday and are attended by myself, the script editor, the production co-ordinator, the story team and the commissioned Writers. Sometimes a writer may want to expand scenes, or bring extra characters in and leave others out. They may want to move a scene to another location – and that is when the conference room turns into a trading fair, with people asking who will swap a location scene for a Rovers, or who can afford to lose a couple of scenes. Each writer likes to mould the story to suit their own requirements, and as long as they take it from A to B and pass it on to the next writer with no gaps in continuity, then some leeway is acceptable. Turning the basic storyline documents into quality *Coronation Street* scripts is probably one of the hardest jobs imaginable.

Left: David has a meeting with director Ged Maguire.
Centre: Watching the filming with director Garth Tucker.
Right: Amending a script.

'Coronation Street is the biggest programme in Britain – it's my mum's favourite programme and I've grown up with it.'

Ultimately, *Coronation Street* is only as good as its scripts. Of course, to maintain its high standards, good performances, good direction and good production values are also essential. But the script is the starting point, and if the writing doesn't convince, the finished product will be lacking.

Almost everyone in television production starts out with a script in front of them. Directors, actors, cameramen – each and every person involved from start to finish is given a script and can make decisions about how to direct a scene, play a scene or shoot a scene on the basis of the written word. However, for every episode of *Coronation Street* that is ever made, just one person has to sit down alone with a blank piece of paper or word-processing screen, and spend two weeks putting words into the mouths of the most famous characters in Britain.

Most producers are constantly on the lookout for new writers, liking to nurture new talent and keep refreshing their regular team. But becoming a writer on the *Street* must be one of the most daunting career prospects ever. It is certainly a lengthy process. As well as meeting people from agencies, or film schools, a lot of people send us scripts on spec. Myself, Carolyn Reynolds and script editor Pamela Woods try to read as many as possible, although there is always a huge backlog. Out of the hundreds of scripts we get, just a few may be worth following up, but even then there is a long way to go before joining the team.

A potential scriptwriter will be invited to story conferences for several weeks to sit in and listen and get to know the show and the characters. Once they feel comfortable they will be invited to submit a shadow script, based on storylines from an episode already transmitted. After that has been approved they will be asked to write an actual episode and if that works out they may be commissioned again, but it takes a while to become part of the established team of a dozen or so regulars.

Sometimes the story conference alone is enough to put people off. It is a trial by fire, and people have been known in the past to turn up to one meeting and never appear again. 'It was very frightening,' recalls Joe Turner, who has been writing for the programme for a year now. 'At my first conference I didn't contribute much at all – it was six months before I finally had the courage to finally contribute a fully worked out idea.'

Despite previous writing experience which included *Children's Ward*, *Holby City* and the award winning children's programme *My Dad's a Boring Nerd*, Joe initially found writing for *Coronation Street* awe-inspiring.

Storyliner Stephen Hughes works on a future episode.

'*Coronation Street* is the biggest programme in Britain – it's my mum's favourite and I've grown up with it.' he says. 'From that point of view it was terrifying, but it's an honour and a privilege to be a part of it, and it was very exciting when the first episode I ever wrote was transmitted and I saw my name come up over the cobbled street after the titles.'

It's no wonder that fresh faces are intimidated, though. Some of the more established scribes on the programme have been around for over twenty years, and know the characters as well as they know themselves.

John Stevenson, whose first *Coronation Street* episode was transmitted in January 1976, concedes that it can be difficult. 'You have to hit the ground running with this show,' he says. 'It is very hard to come into it as a new person and it's no wonder that some

don't manage it. You have to keep all the characters' individual voices in your head, and you really need to have an ear for it. A lot of very good writers want to work for *Coronation Street* but when they do a sample script it doesn't sound right, because people don't speak the way they should do.'

Maintaining a naturalistic dialogue is of paramount importance – and the more skilled the writer, the more believable the characters sound. 'It's a very artificial structure, as is all drama, and the more realistic it looks, the more artifice has gone into it,' adds John. 'The effect you want is of the actors making up their lines as they go along. And quite intelligent people have said to us, "Do you go along with a notebook and listen to the actors talking?" It's amazing, but you don't want the viewers to ever notice the writing or direction. You want them to think there is just a camera unobtrusively clocking these people, and a microphone listening to what they say.'

It is also vitally important to love the characters – even the nasty ones. Writing in a hostile way is a mistake, because even bad characters don't think of themselves that way, and it is vital to write from their point of view. If this rule is ignored, the viewers lose patience, and the programme quickly becomes melodrama, rather than emotional truth.

'It is the job of the writer on a show like this to make people believe in the characters' humanity,' John continues. 'Rationally, we know that other people are as alive as us, but emotionally we don't. It's only when you feel someone else's joy or pain and have that empathy that you understand you are not the only person in the world.

'Hayley is a very good example. We wanted to make people see what it would be like to be her, whatever their views on transsexuals. If you can get even one person in the audience to feel how it is to get up in the morning and be someone else, then that is a great achievement.'

Caring doesn't mean giving characters an easy ride, though, and the reason that so many people in a soap lead such a miserable

Right: Mariam
Vossough (left) and
Diane Burrows
discuss plotlines.

existence is that conflict is more entertaining than consensus. The best *Coronation Street* episodes are ones that combine high drama with comic scenes, but despite the comedy, few Weatherfield residents have trouble-free lives. Most viewers believe that they want the *Street* to stay the same, and prefer people to be happy, but the truth is that happy endings are boring, and if there are no problems to be resolved, there's no story either.

When scripts are finished there is more tweaking to be done. First drafts arrive in buff copies and are sent to me and script editor Pamela Woods. We make notes, and then have a long editing session. I may ask for changes to scenes that I feel aren't right. Sometimes it's nothing specific; just the idea that something could be reworked to make it funnier. Or sometimes there may simply be too many swear words or violence for a 7.30pm audience, and I'll decide what should be removed.

Pamela studies the scripts for continuity, and liaises with the writers. Sometimes, despite the commissioning conference, a writer may submit something that is completely different from what was

in the storylines. If it's really good, it will be kept in, but it might disrupt the next few episodes and cause problems for the other writers. With eight different individuals on board it is vital to ensure that the scripts match up and it is Pamela's job to make them cohere.

More archive material is also fed in at this stage. If, for example, a character is discussing an issue such as abortion, Pamela would check with Daran to see if they have any particular attitude historically. If there has been an abortion in that family in the past and the character involved suddenly takes a different position now, we would have to justify that or alter their opinions.

Daran also writes diverse little notes along the lines of 'Eunice Gee's boarders don't have their own toilets,' 'Sharon Gaskell is an Aries, not a Capricorn,' or 'She was called Dolly, not Mabel,' referring to a character from the distant past. It sounds incredibly pernickety, but *Coronation Street* has such a dedicated fan base that if just one detail were to be misremembered, there would be an immediate hail of complaints from disgruntled viewers. Finally, the legal department make sure we haven't mentioned brand names,

'It's seductive to write for *Coronation Street* because you know 18 million people will see your work. And by and large it's possible to work on this show and be really proud of it.'

and aren't in breach of ITC regulations. Each script has to be checked for libel and slander and for copyright issues if a piece of poetry or music is used.

It is at this stage that new writers sometimes need extra assistance. 'Often they don't quite know the characters, and I'd have to point out that Roy Cropper is too well read to make a certain mistake, or Les Battersby isn't clever enough to use such a long word,' Pamela explains. 'I might initially go through and add catch-phrases, such as Fred's "I say!" to capture a character's voice, but after five or six episodes the writers begin to hear the voices more clearly for themselves.'

Writing for *Coronation Street* is a brutal process. With four episodes a week to be processed, there is little time to keep reworking a script if a writer falls ill, has writer's block, or just gets it wrong. It is extremely exacting even for established writers, but new writers can find it terrifying, as there is no room for failure.

Add to this unavoidable dramas such as actors going off sick and episodes having to be rewritten virtually the night before filming,

and you get some idea of the pressure put on the team. But there are also benefits. 'If you are a writer, you want to be read, heard or seen,' says John Stevenson. 'It's seductive to write for *Coronation Street* because you know 18 million people will see your work. And by and large it's possible to work on this show and be really proud of it.'

2
the
Creating
Characters

The Casting Department

Think back to some of the most memorable *Coronation Street* characters over the years, and you would find it hard to imagine them played by any other actors. To the vast army of fans, many of whom have tuned in to the programme since the very beginning, Pat Phoenix *was* Elsie Tanner, and Hilda Ogden could never have been captured as perfectly by anyone other than the wonderful Jean Alexander.

Today's characters are the same. Bill Tarmey and Liz Dawn are ideal as Jack and Vera Duckworth, and the Rovers bar wouldn't be the same place without Betty Driver's presence as the formidable Betty Williams. Even some of the newer faces seem to have fitted into the *Street* for ever – long-term writer Peter Whalley immediately took to Alan Halsall and, after watching an early episode featuring him as the troublesome Tyrone, he was heard to declare that *Coronation Street* had found 'the young Albert Tatlock'.

Yet at one time all of the now-familiar and well-loved faces had to be chosen from a vast pool of available talent. And there is a tremendous pressure to get it right. Choosing the ideal actor or actress can bring a character vividly to life, often for years to come – but picking the wrong person for a role can sadly lead to the character's early demise.

New characters begin their life in story conferences where they are initially shaped by the imaginations of the writers. Many of the most memorable arise naturally from the storylines. Danny Hargreaves was introduced after it was decided that Sally should take a market stall as part of her attempt to rebuild her life after Greg Kelly. Once the market setting was established, someone suggested it would be a good idea if she met a nice man there, and Danny was created. Or we may be actively seeking someone to play against a current character who is becoming isolated. We re-introduced Tracie Bennett as Sharon Gaskell because, following the departures of Mavis Wilton and Alec Gilroy, we needed to find a relationship for Rita, and fortunately Tracie was available. Meg Johnson as Eunice Gee is another face from the past – but in the vast majority of cases, we start the search from scratch.

Senior casting director Judi Hayfield and casting director June West regularly attend the story conferences in order to determine the profiles of newly introduced characters. A general idea of the person required will come out of the discussions between writers and storyliners. Certain factors will be established before the auditions can begin. How old is a character? Are they down to earth or larger than life? Sympathetic or nasty? Refined or rough and ready? To avoid making mistakes later on, everything is noted down and taken into account, and of course each person involved in the casting process will also add his or her own perspective.

On occasions we also require a specific look. When we introduced Rovers barmaid Samantha Failsworth, it had been dictated in the story conference that she would be aloof but attractive to men. The hunt was on for an extremely good-looking girl and we eventually chose Tina Hobley. But it isn't an exact science. If we need to cast a handsome young man, Judi and June will obviously know who is appealing, but the character has to be popular with men as well so it isn't just a case of picking the best looker. Looks are subjective, anyway, and at the end of the day a lot boils down to personal taste.

Sometimes, if it is felt that an actor is absolutely right for a role, notes on appearances can be overruled. The first example of this occurred way back in 1960 when casting for the original characters took place. Tony Warren, *Coronation Street*'s original creator, had always envisaged Ena Sharples as being thin and scrawny, but after a fruitless search for an actress who answered this description, he changed his mind and approached the solidly built Violet Carson. She then went on to make hairnetted

Waiting to go on set – Bill Tarmey and Chris Canavan (right).

Ena the greatest malevolent matriarch the programme has ever had. No doubt there have been countless other reversals since.

Of course, a hopeful candidate's appearance counts for nothing if they can't play the role convincingly.. With such a demanding show as *Coronation Street* it is always necessary to cast primarily on acting ability. There is simply too much at stake to risk someone not being up to the challenge.

Even with small roles, such as a one-off appearance as a sales assistant or a visiting relative of an established character, the tendency is to 'cast up' rather than choose someone who is merely competent. A seemingly small role in terms of dialogue may be vitally important to the rest of the story. For example, a scene in which Jack Duckworth is told he has a heart condition depends on the skill of the actor playing the doctor, as his role involves imparting vital information to a much-loved character that the audience really cares about.

There is huge pressure to find new talent on a continual basis. As well as the regular characters there are usually at least six small parts a week being cast, and great care is taken to choose the best possible person for each. Judi and June are rarely off duty, and as well as visiting drama schools they spend most of their evenings sitting in theatres up and down the country, seeing as many

performances as possible, making notes, and keeping an eye on new talent.

Even watching television turns into a professional activity rather than a relaxing night in front of the box. 'It's a bonus if I enjoy something I see, but basically I tend to look at the actors,' says June. 'I thought of auditioning Richard Standing for the role of Danny after seeing him in *Picking Up the Pieces* and *The Grand*, and I spotted Ian Mercer, who plays Gary Mallet, in *Cracker*. Casting is about finding new talent and bringing it in, and your knowledge grows with the amount of actors you know.'

Sometimes the process can be very fast – June may phone me and say, 'How about so and so for this character?', and if I know

'I think the regular cast are flattered by the calibre of the guest actors. It lifts them up and refreshes their performances.'

their work and think they would be good then we'll simply check their availability. More often candidates are auditioned from a small shortlist. Over the years relatively minor roles have been played by some of the best actors this country has produced. Prunella Scales, Paula Wilcox, Joanna Lumley, Richard Beckinsale, Martin Shaw, Warren Clarke and Mollie Sugden are just a few of the famous faces who have taken tiny parts on *Coronation Street*. Even Ben Kingsley appeared in a few episodes playing a man who took a fancy to Ken's sister-in-law, Irma Barlow.

'I think the regular cast are flattered by the calibre of the guest actors,' says Judi Hayfield. 'It lifts them up and refreshes their performances.' Needless to say, even more care is taken with long-term characters, and some marvellous people have joined the cast over the last few years.

Occasionally good actors will audition and even win small parts in the *Street*, but it may be years before they find the right niche, the character they can really make their own. Sean Wilson auditioned for the roles of Terry Duckworth and Curly Watts before being cast as Martin Platt, and Roy Barraclough and Bill Waddington each took four different minor parts on the programme before coming in to play Alec and Percy.

'The regulars get a huge buzz out of a new actor coming in – particularly if they are going to be working with them on a particular story,' adds Judi. 'New people are always bowled over at how welcome they are made, and how much people are prepared to help them. It is wonderful when we have somebody like David Neilson [Roy Cropper] in the show, who has been working solidly for years and brings all that skill, expertise and credibility with him, and there are a great many actors in *Coronation Street* who have very good track records.'

Several of the cast were already very well known when they came into the programme, but such is the kudos of *Corrie* that even very well-established stars often want to be a part of it. Denise Welch, now landlady of the Rovers, began writing to Judi Hayfield for a part on the *Street* as soon as she left drama school, and by the time the opportunity to play Natalie arose she was already famous for her role in *Soldier Soldier*. Jonathan Guy Lewis from *London's Burning* had a high profile when he was cast as Ian Bentley but was desperate to appear in the *Street*.

But there is no hard and fast rule to say that newcomers to the business can't be just as impressive. 'Casting *Coronation Street* is very different to anything else,' says Judi Hayfield. 'The programme has been around for such a long time and it does have a very particular chemistry of its own. You may see somebody who has a really solid background at the National or the RSC and they will be very good actors, but they may come into the *Street* and not feel real. Then again you could get someone who is brilliant in *Coronation Street* but who would not have the range to be cast elsewhere.'

It has been well documented that several of *Coronation Street*'s most consistently popular artists have backgrounds in cabaret, rather than drama school. Bill Tarmey and Liz Dawn both had singing careers and had worked as extras before landing their roles as Jack and Vera Duckworth, and both are utterly convincing and always lend the right weight and emotion to a scene.

One of the biggest problems can be casting the younger characters. There is no lengthy rehearsal time in which to perfect performances, and for relatively inexperienced actors this can be a problem, as there's no room to make mistakes.

'It's very difficult to come into this show because you have to find your feet from day one, and we have enormous problems getting young actors who immediately come up to the writers' expectations in terms of performance,' says Judi. 'It's hard, but it's a great show for breeding talent and watching people grow, and there are a lot of people around to learn from. And it's wonderful when you get someone like Georgia Taylor [Toyah] who had very

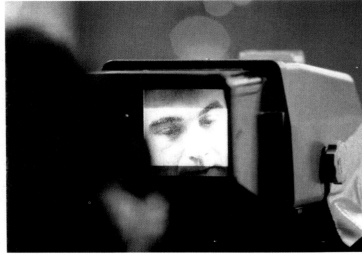

little experience when she came into the show but is a huge find – bright, intelligent and committed.'

As producer, I tend to get very involved in casting, because I prefer not to see anyone on screen that I haven't personally approved. On occasions it isn't possible for me to attend the actual auditions, but in those cases I will usually be given photographs or a tape of the person. With major characters, I always make the time to meet actors personally.

For long-term characters the net is usually spread very widely. The casting directors hold the initial auditions, seeing as many people as possible, and from these there will usually be a shortlist of three or four of the strongest candidates. At this stage, I add my input, as does the director who will be working at the time of the character's first appearance. Executive producer Carolyn Reynolds also gets involved when major characters are being cast. Occasionally the writers will offer an opinion – they may have a person in mind for a role, and suggestions are always listened to, and sometimes acted upon. It is a very democratic process. I have the deciding vote, but we usually work things out as a team – and although we have disagreed in the past, we've never actually fallen out.

For some actors, auditioning for *Coronation Street* may represent the opportunity to be catapulted out of obscurity into the limelight. There's always a chance that the character they are hoping to play will in time become the next Rita Sullivan or Bet Gilroy. But despite this – or maybe because of it – we strive to make the auditions as relaxed as possible.

The proceedings begin in the office with an informal chat. We talk about the character and try to explain the part, then we do a reading. At this stage we will have a script available, and a sample of dialogue will have been selected beforehand. June will take the other character's part, or once in a while we will ask another actor to read with them. Occasionally we shoot their auditions on tape to see how they will look on screen and decide from there.

It is at this point that we begin to get interesting ideas from the actors. They bring their own perspective with them and may see something in the character that we haven't yet thought of. After they have read for us they may be asked to go again, perhaps with some suggestions from the director. The whole process takes approximately half an hour, which puts incredible pressure on the actor. It is a very short time in which to give the best impression of themselves, and the stakes are high as it could be the job which changes their life.

Understandably, many of the actors admit to being extremely apprehensive on the day. Tom Wisdom, who plays Tom Ferguson, confesses that he was terrified at his audition, and few people are without nerves as they read their lines. For many, the tremors continue even when they have won the part. Anne Kirkbride has played Deirdre Rachid for over 25 years but still recalls her panic during her first few appearances.

'It was terrifying,' she admits. 'I was only 17 or 18 and I didn't want to be here. I'd been at Oldham Rep and I was very happy there and then suddenly I was in this big television company and I was scared. I just wanted to get it over with and go back to Oldham Rep.'

More than two decades later, Rebecca Sarker, who plays Nita Desai, also experienced new-girl nerves. 'I never really considered myself a big fan – but when I started here I realised I knew all the characters and the storylines,' she says. 'Everything was just so familiar. I had to keep pinching myself – I couldn't believe I was here, talking to people I'd seen on TV for years.'

Settling in can be a fraught process. Almost nobody is prepared for the upheaval that starring in *Coronation Street* can cause, although the casting department do their best to put new cast members in the picture. '*Coronation Street* is a huge commitment and we do find that people have thought hard about it, but even so most people come in and are knocked sideways,' says Judi. New faces are warned of the huge pressures of filming four episodes a week, and the overwhelming glare of press attention. 'We try to paint the blackest scenario imaginable when they get the job,' laughs Judi. 'We tell them about the character, but also about all the things that go with it.'

For those who can cope with the constant scrutiny, though, the rewards are great. Even for the most experienced artists, walking into *Coronation Street* is like walking into a piece of history.

But unlike most plays or dramas where the protagonists' destinies are predetermined and their personalities already decided, *Coronation Street* characters have infinite possibilities. They can continue to grow and develop for as long as they inspire their creators. The writers watch the programme closely, and often pick up on the little idiosyncrasies that the actors bring to their characters.

Jacqueline Pirie who plays Linda Sykes rolls her own cigarettes and this was a trait that her character inherited. Writer Peter Whalley noticed this and wanted her to keep on doing it, even when the downmarket factory lass started living it up as the mistress of Mike Baldwin.

When Roy Cropper first appeared in *Coronation Street* he was perceived as being a bit sinister, yet he needed to be accepted by the other characters if he was to have a future in the show. Then David Neilson introduced the famous shopping bag with the key tied to it – a quirk that he in turn had observed from his own mother. The writers liked what he was doing and were able to add the other endearing layers and peculiarities, and eventually the public fell in love with Roy.

Characters' catchphrases develop in the same way. A writer may repeat something and if the actor likes it they may insert it again later on in the same episode until it eventually becomes a regular feature. Fred Elliott's 'I say' is a classic example. Similarly, if an actor seizes on a funny line, the writers may notice their talent for comic dialogue and write more humorous material for them.

Creating the Characters

The supporting artists are vital to the show.
Top: Lottie Goodwin.
Centre: Chris Canavan.
Bottom: An OSM directs some supporting artists.

'You try to write to the strengths of the actors and ignore their weaknesses,' says John Stevenson. 'Sometimes new people are plunged into a big story straight away, but if you can it's best to bring them in on the fringe of events and have a look at them. Then you can see what they do well and what kinds of things come out in their performance and decide where you should go from there.'

Many of the writers like to meet the actors and talk to them about their characters to reassure themselves that they are thinking along the same lines. Others prefer not to. One ex-writer, Frank Cottrell-Boyce, was always reluctant to meet Sarah Lancashire in case it marred his ability to write for Raquel.

New actors are monitored when they come into the programme. Because *Coronation Street* has such a relentless schedule they have to be up to speed as soon as they begin work. It's like trying to jump aboard a moving train, and while performers may get feedback from individual directors, it's part of a producer's job to keep an eye on them and give an overall picture. I listen to reactions from the studio floor, and try to see the cast regularly. Constant communication is important, and although it isn't possible to see everyone in such a large cast week in and week out, I do encourage them to come up to see me and discuss their characters, as do the casting department.

Although all the attention is inevitably concentrated on the principal artists as far as the press and public are concerned, the background artists or extras also provide a vitally important contribution. They rarely speak on camera but a great deal of care is put into casting the men and women who lend that all-important community feel to *Coronation Street*.

Rather than just adding random people, each location – Underworld, the Rovers Return and Roy's Rolls – has its own group of 'regulars', just as any factory, pub or cafe would in real life. Lists of familiar faces are compiled and rotated. Some are put into couples or groups of friends and often used together, and many of the background artists have been part of the Weatherfield

'There is an art to looking natural as an extra. We are like children – seen and not heard, but we have to remember where to stand and how to move.'

community for longer than the principal cast. For them, *Coronation Street* is far more than just a casual job.

Chris Canavan has been part of the fabric of the programme for 37 years and has had several small speaking parts. Amongst other things, he's been the Ogdens' window cleaner, the Ogdens' mouse catcher, the man who accidentally locked the juvenile Barlow twins in a warehouse and the first ever customer in the Kabin, where he ordered a quarter pound of Everton mints.

Over the decades 71-year-old Chris has seen many changes. 'When I first started I was in rep, as most of the actors had been, and in those days you all spoke very fast and very loud,' he says. 'It's completely changed now with the new techniques, but it's very enjoyable.'

When Chris began working on *Coronation Street*, the rate for supporting artists was five guineas a day, and they were reimbursed immediately. 'You finished work, went upstairs and got paid right away, which was essential because no-one had any money,' he laughs. 'It was very exciting then because you could work on *Coronation Street* until about 2.00pm, go into *Families at War* until 6.00 or 7.00, and then stay in the evening and go into one of the live shows. Bill Podmore once put me in as a sidekick to Arthur English in *How's Your Father*, which was great. I had plenty of dialogue there.'

Another background artist who has become an integral part of the programme is ex-singer Lottie Goodwin. Lottie has been a veteran of the show for 30 years but has no intention of giving up,

even at the age of 87. 'I enjoy it, I must say,' she reveals. 'You meet some nice friends here. You do get a bit bored sometimes, waiting around, but I've got the energy to do it, and it keeps me going.'

They both take a great deal of pride in their roles. 'There is an art to looking natural as an extra. We are like children – seen and not heard, but we have to remember where to stand and how to move,' says Chris. 'You can't work without extras – they are a necessity,' adds Lottie. 'We do our job and we do it well.'

Despite being background artists rather than principals, both Lottie and Chris have been recognized by *Corrie*'s vigilant fans, and even received fan mail. 'I have been asked for my autograph,' says Lottie. 'I say that I'm only a supporting artist, but people say, "As long as you're on *Coronation Street* it doesn't matter." It's remarkable because we're only seen for a flash.'

As well as the regulars, the milkmen, the postmen and the frequent passers-by, there are numerous occasions on which new people are required. 'We look for the right kind of faces, age range and so on,' says June West. 'So if we had scenes in a wine bar or a different pub we'd note down what sort of area it was and the type of clientele they would attract. The vast majority of background artists are hand picked. We generally use people who have had professional experience and we are constantly meeting people. We chat to them about their background, and note down special skills – which can be anything from being able to rollerblade or drive an HGV to playing a musical instrument.'

Once cast, the background artists share the same responsibilities as the other actors. They must be punctual, professional and able to work in any conditions. The hours are long and there is a huge amount of standing round, but their commitment to the show has to be total, just as with the principal artists. Appearing in *Coronation Street* may be a dream role for thousands of aspiring actors and background artists, but it is a huge stage on which to succeed or fail, and carries a great responsibility. Thankfully, over the years the vast majority of *Coronation Street* artists have been more than up to the challenge.

3
Creating
the
Coronation
Street Look

The Costume and Make-up Departments

Most people remember *Dallas* and *Dynasty* from the mid-eighties for the big hair, outrageous shoulder pads and inch-thick perfect make-up while costume dramas require specially made outfits and wigs that closely resemble the fashions from whichever era they are set in. And many successful American sitcoms are a televisual feast of designer clothes and flawless good looks. In the case of *Friends,* the hairstyle of one leading actress started a craze which swept across the Atlantic, with twenty-somethings from New York to Newcastle marching into hairdressers to ask for a graduated, highlighted cut which was known for a whole year as 'the Rachel'. *Coronation Street*, however, set in a working-class suburb of Manchester, simply wouldn't ring true if its characters looked like they'd just stepped off the catwalk.

And as it is set in the present day, there's rarely any need for research into period garments or hairstyles. Instead the challenge is to make the residents of Weatherfield look completely ordinary, like the type of people you might see every day in your local pub or the neighbourhood shops. And it is the job of *Coronation Street*'s costume and make-up departments to ensure that each character on the programme appears convincingly average.

Despite the lack of specialist requirements, though, dressing and styling almost 40 regular cast members, as well as the various occasional characters that wander through the show each week, is a huge task. Although the brief is to keep the characters 'ordinary', each one also has an individual look according to their fictional incomes, personalities and preferences. And it is up to costume designers Michael Blaney and Sandie Hill to stock and maintain their wardrobes.

The costume department in Stage One, the purpose-built home of the indoor sets, fills two large rooms. The men's garments are situated upstairs, and the ladies' outfits are downstairs in the main office, sharing the available space with two desks, a television and a laundry room full of washers and driers. Rows of rails are crammed with costumes. Suits, shirts, scarves and skirts are hung together in a riot of colour. Jeans, jumpers and jackets jostle for space on the crowded hangers. Everything that the characters could possibly need is on display. There are dressing gowns, pyjamas and hats, winter coats and skimpy summer clothes, jewellery and handbags. It's like a sartorial Aladdin's Cave.

To make sure that none of the costumes get mixed up, each section of portable rail is clearly labelled with the character's name, but many of the outfits are so familiar that it's immediately obvious who owns what. Hayley's ubiquitous red anorak hangs alongside her collection of sensible skirts, while Toyah's grey school uniform is next to her combat trousers and tie-dyed T-shirts. Alma's rail is full of smart jackets, while Janice's consists of casual clothes and the overall she wears in the factory. The men's clothes aren't quite as distinctive, but Spider's overgrown woolly jumpers are fairly unique, and provide a stark contrast to Mike Baldwin's sharp suits.

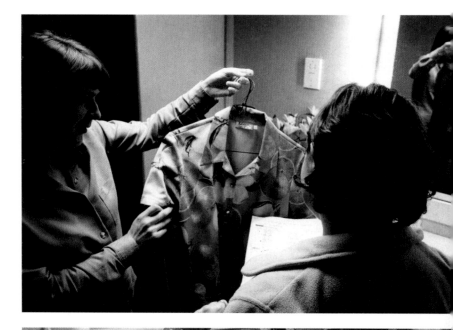

'Even if I'm on holiday I look around the ladies' shops and think, "Oh, that would fit so-and-so."'

There are six people working in the costume department – Michael, Sandie and four dressers – two male and two female. Between them they have to ensure that each and every actor that goes on set literally 'looks the part'. When an actor comes in on a filming day they will find the outfit they are to wear for the next scene hanging on the back of a chair in their dressing room, clean and pressed. If they need to change between scenes they will return to their dressing room to find that the next outfit has also been laid out.

There are usually about four costume changes per character, per day, although because time is tight these are kept to a minimum if possible. The factory girls, for example, wear jeans and overalls most of the time, so often they will be asked to change just their T-shirts rather than donning a whole new outfit. Then, when the actors have finished with the clothes, they can leave them in their dressing rooms, secure in the knowledge that the dressers will collect them and make sure they are washed and ironed ready for the next wear.

The title 'dresser' is actually quite misleading. Unless someone specifically requires assistance, the dressers don't help people in and out of their clothes. 'They do it on other programmes, but we tend not to, because there are so many actors,' explains Michael Blaney. 'When new people come in sometimes they can't understand why they don't get fussed over, but over the years we've learned that it's better and less hassle to just leave people to it, although if people want help they can ask us.'

Instead the dressers have their work cut out making sure everyone has the right outfits, doing alterations and mending, and taking care of the mounds of laundry each week. Often there are

up to three rails full of clothes which all need washing, drying and ironing with a steam iron, as well as incidentals such as the towels from Audrey's salon and tea towels from Roy's Rolls. Occasionally they may also be called upon to create an outfit from scratch. When Hayley got married it stated in the scripts that her dress and those of the bridesmaids were home made, so it was Allen Crawford who got to work with a sewing machine on her behalf.

The department operates on a two-week schedule. Each week one of the costume designers is rostered, along with two dressers on PSC (location) and four on studio days. Meanwhile the other will be on a 'prep' week, making sure they have everything they need for the coming week's filming.

Allen Crawford puts the finishing touches to Hayley's wedding dress.

On the Monday during prep, the rostered designer will read the four scripts for the week ahead and prepare the character sheets, noting down how many outfits each person will need and if there are any specifics. For example, if a script says, 'Nita has just come back from the gym,' they have to ensure that she will be suitably attired. If the character hasn't been seen in trainers and exercise gear before, then a trip to the shops is in order.

Over the next couple of days, some portable rails will be set up for the week's filming. Each character's costumes are hung up, checked and double checked, itemized on a list and then organized according to the filming and studio schedules, which dictate on which day and in which order the scenes are filmed. A list is then given to the dressers, whose responsibility it is to ensure that the right outfit reaches the right dressing room or is brought to a winnebago on location in plenty of time for the actor to change.

Invariably there will be shopping to do. Short-term characters will need outfits, even if they are only making the briefest of appearances, and regular characters require specific items most weeks. At the same time the costume department has to constantly update each character's wardrobe so there are always things to buy. The most hardened shopper would be daunted by the task, although after a while it becomes second nature to keep an eye out for bargains. 'Even if I'm on holiday I look around the ladies' shops and think, "Oh, that would fit so-and-so,"' laughs Michael.

As the brief is to keep the characters looking ordinary, their clothes are simply selected from everyday outlets. The younger characters like Leanne, Toyah and Maxine are given clothes from cheap and cheerful chainstores, while the wealthier, slightly more sophisticated characters like Audrey will be dressed in clothes from more upmarket emporiums. The factory uniforms and cafe aprons come from a specialist shop which supplies work wear, but generally speaking you could probably buy the vast majority of *Corrie*'s clothes in your own high street.

Sometimes the actors go out shopping with the costume designers, but busy schedules usually prohibit this, so Michael or Sandie will set off alone armed with the actor's measurements and relying on experience and guesswork in the absence of anyone to try on the outfits. Anything that doesn't look right will be taken back at a later date.

Even though most of the outfits are intentionally unremarkable, there are sometimes noticeable traits in particular characters' clothing, which the viewing public aren't slow to pick up on. Recently both the costume department and actress Denise Welch have been bombarded with letters commenting on Natalie's tendency to wear sleeveless tops, even in the middle of winter.

'It's never deliberate, it just happens,' says Michael. 'With Natalie, we initially bought a couple of dresses with no sleeves and Denise liked the look. Then the next thing you know, you've bought a top the same and suddenly people are talking about her.'

Just as in real life, though, a character may have a favourite look, whether it is sleeveless tops or the midriff-exposing pink T-shirts Maxine is often seen in. And sometimes it becomes their trademark. Liz McDonald was well known for her short skirts, and when actress Beverly Callard left the programme she was presented with a framed black lycra miniskirt as a memento. Percy Sugden was rarely seen without a flat cap, and the name Bet Gilroy was synonymous with fake leopardskin. Raquel had her own unique over-the-top style, never deviating from the colourful tight tops and perilously high stilettos, even when the rest of the world were wearing sober neutrals and platform trainers.

Coronation Street fans take an active interest in the actors' apparel, and often try to contribute. Julie Goodyear was constantly receiving enormous plastic earrings from viewers hoping to see their gifts dangling from Bet's ears on screen, and Elizabeth Bradley is often sent hats for Maud Grimes. We don't need to worry about Roy Cropper losing his trademark grey shopping bag either, as David Neilson has been given several spares. New babies also inspire gifts, and several outfits were donated after the Mallet twins were born.

'Kevin Webster has had the same leather jacket since the day he arrived 16 years ago!'

As well as individuals, companies are keen to see their clothes on *Coronation Street*. However, we have to be very careful about what we accept, and we can't use anything with a prominent brand name or a very distinctive logo. On a purely practical level, we also tend to avoid too much white, which gives off glare, and checks and stripes are approached with caution because they can cause strobing on camera.

For every person wanting to send something in to the show, there are many more desperate to take away a souvenir. Every week letters arrive from hopeful viewers asking if they can have Jack Duckworth's old glasses or Hilda's headscarves.

'We get them all the time, especially after weddings,' says Michael. 'They want to know where the dress came from, or where a tiara came from. We get hundreds of letters saying, "My daughter is getting married soon and she's the same size, so can she have the dress?" We got one asking for Judy Mallet's maternity frock recently so I put it in an envelope and sent it, but most of the things that people ask for we can't give away.'

If a major new character comes into the programme their image has to be determined from scratch. I will have meetings with the costume designers about the kind of look we want for that person, and any direct specifications are handed down even before their first T-shirt has been purchased. Even once the character has been around for a while, I keep a careful eye on their image – often getting involved to the extent of going down to the costume department and removing any clothes that I don't like from the rails.

Some characters' looks are more specific than others. We knew that Spider Nugent was an eco-warrior and would dress accordingly, and over the years the occasional character of Tracy Barlow has developed a passion for grunge chic. Usually, though, the guidelines for the costume department are based around practicalities such as a character's income and what they do for a living.

Once the role has been cast the costume designers will usually meet the actor, talk to them and take their measurements, before discussing what type of wardrobe to buy. With an important character, Sandie and Michael will go shopping together. For

minor ones, whoever is on duty that week will take care of things.

Sometimes there can be problems. 'When Tom came in we didn't have time to meet him beforehand, and even though we had his measurements we didn't expect him to be quite so tall,' explains Michael. 'We'd been told his character would be a bit Boyzone-ish, so we bought him loads of sleeveless tops which looked wrong, and we also put him in red which is a colour that doesn't suit him, but by then it was too late.' I agreed that Tom needed a change, so over the next few weeks his image was gradually altered, but thankfully mistakes are few and far between.

Often a character will begin with one look and change as the character mellows. When the Battersby girls first arrived, their wardrobe was horrendous and their make-up deliberately tacky. Jane Danson in particular hated Leanne's 'Spice Girl' hairstyle which was brown with two red streaks in the front, but as the girls matured and settled down, their make-up and fashion sense improved slightly – although not much! Spider, on the other hand,

hasn't had any new clothes since he arrived although his hairstyle has become less extreme. 'He's not a "new clothes" person,' reasons Michael. 'He just wears T-shirts, jumpers and scruffy trousers. And Kevin Webster has had the same leather jacket since the day he arrived 16 years ago! Michael Le Vell often points out to me that he's never been bought a new coat.'

At the moment, Rita, Audrey and Alma own the biggest wardrobes on the *Street*, but the rails are constantly being cleared out as actors' sizes change or clothes become too unfashionable or simply worn out. Discarded clothes are stored in a room upstairs and some are given away for charity auctions or competition prizes. It's very rare for the actors to become attached to the clothes and ask to keep them.

'I think they're glad to get them off,' jokes Michael. 'Julie Hesmondhalgh likes Hayley's red coat but that's just because her mum has got one. One of the first things she told me was that if her mum likes what she's wearing on screen she knows we've got it

right for Hayley. But we buy clothes for the character, not the actor, and I'm sure half of them don't like what they wear.'

Once the clothes have been sorted out, there is make-up and hair to be taken care of. Each week, one of the two make-up designers, Linda Strath and Jane Hatch, plus a team of make-up artists (usually two on PSC and four or five in studio) are there to ensure that everyone who goes on set is made up correctly. On a filming week the rostered team will be there from first call – often as early as 6.45am – until the end of the day, but like the costume department they also have to have several days for preparation – reading scripts, schedules and writing up notes for the week ahead. 'People always say "What do you need the scripts for?" but there's more to it than people realize,' says Linda Strath. 'You have to establish whether characters are looking glamorous for a night out or if they've just got out of bed or whatever. Then we buy the general make-up items that we need, or occasionally something more specific like a wig or glitter eyeshadow, and that all usually takes about three days.'

Next the make-up designer has to sort out the actors' call times with the first assistant director. The first works out approximately what time actors are required for their first scene of the day and the make-up designer adds on the amount of time they will need to spend in make-up. Generally the men need about half an hour unless they are to have their hair washed and styled, and the female cast members take anything up to an hour, depending on how much make-up they wear and whether they use a wig. Most of the cast pass through the make-up department on filming days, although a minority, including Anne Kirkbride, prefer to do their own faces.

After the call times are sorted out, a rota is drawn up from the schedules and each make-up girl is assigned a list of artists. As well as the initial make-ups, which are staggered throughout the day, there may also be changes between scenes – for example, from a casual daytime look to an evening look – so the department is always busy.

Throughout the day the designer and a couple of assistants are

on hand to greet the actors as they come in and get them ready. Usually they are the first contact point of the day for an artist, so as well as their styling skills the girls need to have a friendly and reassuring manner. Often the room is as busy as a railway station with people rushing in to have their hair put up or taken down, lipstick changed or eyeshadow reapplied. But although the faces being made up are some of the most famous in Britain and despite the pressure to dash out and complete the day's filming, the atmosphere is one of friendly banter and gossip just like you might find in any local salon.

The make-up department is situated on the second floor in Stage One. The brightly lit, spotlessly clean room is home to a cornucopia of beauty products. There is also a waiting area to one side of the room – a small alcove with comfy couches, a television, water cooler and tea and coffee machine. A nearby noticeboard is crammed with schedules and rosters, and on the table is a plastic album filled with polaroid photographs. Larger framed photographs of cast past and present adorn the walls.

To the left by the entrance there is a small hairdressing area complete with two backwash sinks, three professional hairdryers and two separate styling areas. Round the corner, eight adjustable make-up chairs are arranged in sets of four in front of brightly lit mirrors. Each place is neatly laid out with all the paraphernalia of the trade. Tissues, towels, brushes, rollers, hairspray, cleansers and cotton wool are all kept to hand. Each make-up artist has their own kit full of products, but because *Coronation Street* has such a large cast, each female character also has her own personalized box full of make-up, and there are separate boxes of base colours for the boys.

While half the team are busy upstairs, a couple of other assistants will be standing by on the studio floor or on location. They keep a careful eye on the proceedings and are ready to step in if any of the artists need their hair straightening or lipstick reapplying before a take.

Quite often if a scene begins outside and continues indoors, make-up and costume need to ensure there is direct continuity between PSC and studio, even though the two segments will have

been filmed on different days. In this case polaroids are taken and notes made to ensure that nobody ever walks into the Rovers with a completely different hairstyle from the one they were sporting ten seconds ago outside the door. If a lot of continuity is needed over an episode, the photographs are kept in an album labelled with episode and scene numbers, so if a different person is on duty they have a reliable reference point from which to work.

Most of the make-ups are quite basic, again emphasizing the everyday image of *Coronation Street*. But there are some special cases. Several of the ladies wear wigs – Elizabeth Dawn is transformed into Vera by putting the famous permed wig over her own neat crop, and Julie Hesmondhalgh has short blonde hair under Hayley's brunette pudding-basin style. The wigs take about

20 minutes to put on, and if an actress has longer hair it also has to be pincurled beforehand. Hayley recently had a new style ordered as the character is becoming slightly more adventurous, but the wigs have to be replaced every few months anyway as they fade under the studio lights and become worn from continual washing and styling.

When characters leave, old wigs are kept in storage. The main Granada make-up department across the road from Stage One has a huge stock that can be cut or coloured as necessary. Often these spares come in handy when stunt doubles are used and need to have the same hairstyle as the artist they are standing in for.

Some stunts such as fights or accidents can also require special make-up, and this is an opportunity for the team to be creative. Cuts and bruises are concocted with a palette of colours, which change over time as the bruises grow older. Scabs can be made out of everyday items such as tea leaves and even coffee granules, and burns can be fashioned out of wax or a gelatine and water mix before being coloured in to look effective.

On most days, though, the makeovers are straightforward. The men just have their blemishes covered over, and quite a few of the women are also given a natural look. Some people fare worse than others in the make-up chair, and that is all down to character. So

whereas Natalie and Alma are made to look quite glamorous, poor Toyah is usually relegated to the chipped nail polish look.

Any image changes on the part of the artists have to be discussed with the make-up department and ultimately me if it's a drastic alteration. Sometimes it can be incorporated into the script, with someone announcing they are going for a restyle in the salon and emerging with a new hairdo, but if any of the actors suddenly wanted to start sporting dreadlocks or a mohican, the answer would almost definitely be no! While the artists are free to look as glamorous or outrageous as they like off screen, the watchword in *Coronation Street* is 'ordinary'. And although *Coronation Street* is unlikely to spark off any major movements in the hair and fashion industries, it is this carefully cultivated normality which makes it so convincing to the viewer.

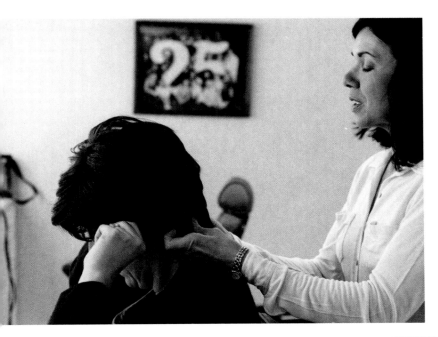

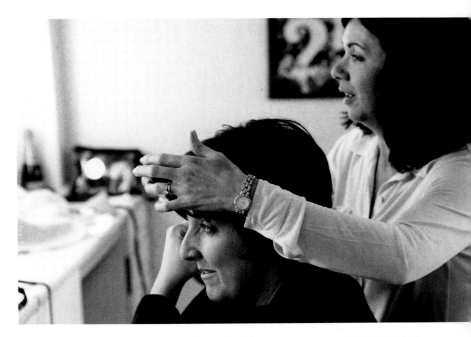

Linda Strath
transforms Julie
Hesmondhalgh
into Hayley
Cropper.

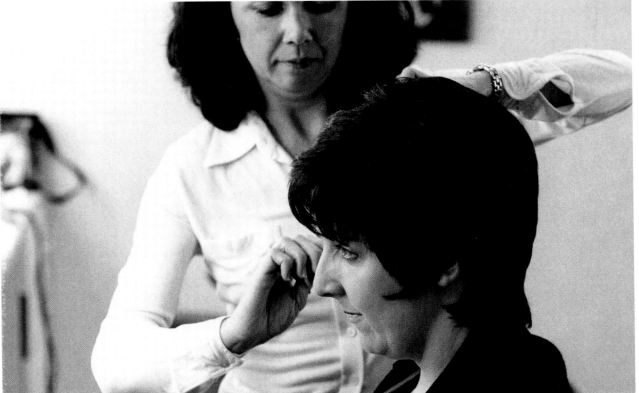

4
Making
the
Street

The Design Department

Coronation Street has come a long way since the old days when all the sets for the week, including the frontage of the famous terraces, were constructed in whatever space was available in the main studios. In those days rehearsals took place in an empty room with lines marked on the floor to denote where the furniture should be.

Inside the design office.

It was years before there was any outdoor set at all, and even then the initial street, built in 1968 and surrounding a railway arch on land leased from the local authority, merely consisted of façades under a half-built roof which were open to all weathers. Space was at a premium on the cold dismal lot and each house was only six feet across, and had to be made to look larger with clever camera angles.

Now the programme has a purpose-built home in Stage One. An enormous studio, opened in 1990, houses the kitchens and living rooms of the *Corrie* characters as well as the famous Rovers, Kabin, Corner Shop and Roy's Rolls. Immediately outside Stage One is the new, improved and much larger street set, built in conjunction with Granada Studio Tours. Doris Speed laid the first foundation stone on 3 December 1981, and the Queen opened the new street in May 1982. When cast and crew aren't filming on the lot, the street doubles up as a popular tourist attraction – and around the corner the original set still stands, transformed into a mock New York street which forms the entrance to the tours.

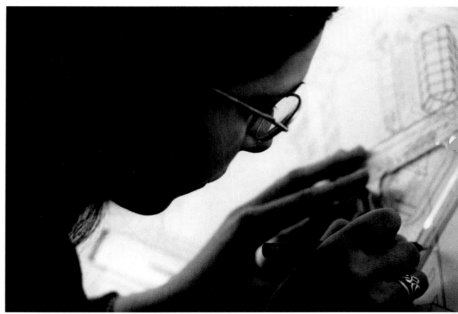

Today's authentically cobbled Coronation Street is home to entire houses, lovingly recreated from reclaimed Salford brick and complete with back yards. On the other side of the road are the newer dwellings, numbers 4, 6 and 8 – owned by Fred Elliott, Natalie Barnes and the Platts respectively. Local business is flourishing too, with Underworld, Audrey's hair salon and Kevin's garage joining the shops and cafes. Today's Coronation Street even boasts a working postbox which visitors to the tours can use to send their souvenir *Street* postcards, which will arrive on friends' and families' mats complete with a Weatherfield postmark.

The street has certainly changed since its beginnings in 1960, but as the programme constantly grows, so does the demand for sets. Weatherfield is continually expanding even today. There are currently plans underway to extend the outdoor areas as a joint venture with Granada Studio Tours. Soon a new road, Victoria Street, will be springing up around the corner from Coronation Street to house Roy's Rolls, a hardware shop, and quite possibly a

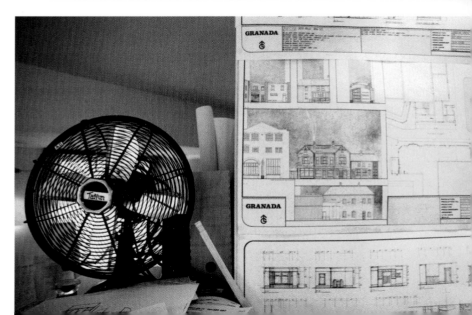

doctors', builder's merchants, a permanent market site and some gates to the brewery. The possibilities are endless.

Any new sets, indoors or out, have to be created from scratch. Whenever a script demands scenes in a room that hasn't been seen before, it is up to production designer Julian Perkins and his team to make the fictional place a reality.

Ideally the design department need to be told as soon as possible if a new set is to be introduced, to allow time for research, design, building, decorating and shopping for accessories. But, as always with a fast-moving drama like *Coronation Street,* time tends to be tight and sometimes a set has to be created very quickly. For a major new location I will sit down with Julian and discuss the overall look beforehand. When Roy's Rolls was redecorated I specified that the cafe should look as if it had been up for years, because although it was a new venture for Roy, it is still an old back street place rather than a brand new cafe bar. After that, the details were left to the design team.

It's important to resist the temptation to go too upmarket, and Roy's Rolls is my idea of a great, traditional *Coronation Street* set.

Although it would be easier to make all the sets look fantastic, it is important to bear in mind that families like the Mallets and the Battersbys would have neither the income nor the imagination to create 'ideal home'-style interiors. If the rooms look slightly shabby it is inevitably the result of hard work and meticulous planning rather than an accident. In fact, *Coronation Street's* most enduringly famous and well-loved set will always be Hilda's living room with its monstrous 'murial' and her forever flying trio of ducks.

For many years the ducks flew across the room, with the middle duck always hanging at a crooked angle. Often a new and inexperienced stage hand would try to straighten it, only to be reprimanded by Jean Alexander who insisted that the creature stayed the way it was.

Attention to detail is very important on *Coronation Street,* and the design team go to great lengths to make the sets look authentic. When new sets are introduced at script level there is usually a stage direction and some form of description from the writer which Julian and his assistants Martin Fitzpatrick and Victoria Cutts interpret for themselves. If the set belongs to a newcomer, Julian

will also call the storyline office to talk to someone who has helped to mould the character and find out their income, occupation and what kind of taste they are likely to have.

When Natalie took over the pub from Jack and Vera, it was obvious that she'd decide to decorate, at least in her own living quarters. As a relatively affluent *Street* character, with two businesses and the income from two properties behind her, Natalie was never going to stand for the old-fashioned, fussy look her predecessors liked. So the Rovers' back room was given the kind of makeover it hasn't seen since before Annie Walker's day. Suddenly the familiar set was modernized, with brighter walls, a new fireplace and more upmarket accessories – although the pub itself was left alone and retains its dingy but homely 'local' atmosphere.

On the other hand, when the Mallets moved into No.9, they were thrilled with the Duckworth decor. Judy and Gary could almost be younger versions of Jack and Vera themselves, so it was decided that they would keep the multicoloured stone cladding which would surely trigger off a barrage of complaints to the council in any other street but Coronation Street. Even the minibar that taste forgot was welcomed by the couple, and since then they've proved that they too have unique interior design skills, adding purple walls and a bizarre trio of flying saucers in the hall.

Once a set has been designed, the construction team headed by Sam Exton work to Julian's specifications to get it ready. If you've ever spent months putting off those tiny DIY jobs, bear in mind that the *Coronation Street* sets often have to be knocked together in just a couple of weeks from start to finish.

There are no ceilings on the interior sets, and the walls that look so solid on screen are actually flat pieces of fabricated timber, manufactured in pieces and then numbered. The modular sections are designed so that they are small enough to carry and can be split up and taken in or out as necessary, without disturbing the other pieces. Everything is designed so that the joints are hidden, and then the flat pieces are held together with special clips. Windows are often made of perspex due to health and safety regulations, and

sometimes they are simply empty frames that can be used as camera traps to film through. When real glass is required, *Coronation Street* uses safety glass, treated with a special film.

At one time all construction work was contracted out, but recently it has been brought in-house, so that changes can be made as necessary. The result has been better-quality sets, and less scope for mistakes.

When the basic set is up with the walls and doors in place and any cupboards, sinks or windows fitted, the decorator has a couple of days to personalize it. He puts up wallpaper, tiles or paints the set in whichever style Julian specifies. Props buyer John Eccles will have been out to buy the materials beforehand. An average set

Top: A model *Street*.

Above: A selection of props – including the stand-ins for the Mallet babies.

The salon set.

sets are dismantled and taken out and new sets for the week ahead are brought over from a huge props storeroom in the bonded warehouse. Once the sets are in place and have been touched up by the decorators, the furniture is brought in and the props laid out.

The only sets that are granted permanent homes in Stage One are communal ones which are used in virtually every episode. The Rovers Return, Roy's Rolls, the Kabin and the Corner Shop are constants, with the others making regular guest appearances in the vast soundproofed space.

Sam Exton draws up a positional floor plan of the studio four weeks in advance detailing which sets are going in and where. These are distributed to the director, first assistant director, production executive, production assistant, design and props, lighting and cameras, and used as a reference point by everybody. The director uses them to help plan camera shots, the first assistant looks at them to determine the flow of studio, as well as making sure they comply with fire and safety regulations, and the technical people determine how the sets will be lit and where to position equipment.

Once the sets are up and decorated and the lighting scaffolding in place, set dressers Jim Coyle and Jim Sulway get to work. Before filming can begin in studio, they have to lay the carpets and hang the curtains or blinds, position furniture and put up pictures, posters or children's drawings. They set out cushions and kitchenware, lamps and ornaments, rugs and mirrors, until the makeshift homes start to take shape. Photographs are regularly taken of the sets to establish exactly where each item belongs, but the team are so experienced that they often know the layout of the rooms without even checking.

Walking through the empty studio is a surreal experience. The homes that seem so familiar on television are much smaller and shabbier in real life, and are arranged side by side amidst a clutter of camera equipment, lighting and props. Doors open abruptly on to the back of another set where you imagine a kitchen or hallway to be; staircases to nowhere end after a few steps; walls are missing

requires about eight rolls of wallpaper, but John will buy three times as many, because the sets are constantly being moved in and out of studio and the walls become scratched and damaged. The sets need constant retouching so it makes sense to buy spare stock at the outset as wallpapers tend to be discontinued after a while, making them difficult to match up.

Even though the studios in Stage One have recently been expanded, there still isn't room to simultaneously house the 30 or so room sets used on *Coronation Street*. Despite the comparative luxury of having an entire studio devoted to just one programme, the sets still have to be rotated as necessary. Each weekend the old

and carpets may have been taken up to accommodate tracks for cameras. Even the furniture seems smaller, and the rooms look crowded. This is intentional because on television the main focus tends to be on talking heads, so sets are deliberately overdressed as a lot of detail in the background helps to establish where the characters are.

On screen, though, it all looks convincing – and this is largely thanks to the diligence of the design and props departments. Everything you see on the programme has to be thought about beforehand and procured from somewhere, and as there is no time during filming days to go looking for props, it all has to be to hand. Each week a props list is compiled which encompasses everything from the mundane to the bizarre, from doughnuts for the cafe to a didgeridoo for Spider.

A lot of the things on the list are established, run of the mill items – Toyah's school bag, Mike Baldwin's briefcase, Maud's wheelchair. These regular props are kept in storage and taken out as needed. Other preparations are the same each week. It would be a disaster if the Rovers were to run out of beer, so Jim makes up all the beverages beforehand – most of which are 100% alcohol free.

The Websters' set is dressed.

'I get letters from viewers asking where they can buy curtains and things.'

The Rovers' beer is actually shandy, and their lager is shandy diluted with lemonade to make it a little paler. Brandy, whisky and other dark spirits consist of burnt sugar and water, and the clear spirits like Bacardi or vodka are just water. White wine is water with lime juice added to tint it and red wine is made from Vimto. Occasionally the drinks are altered to suit the actors' tastes. One actress was allergic to Vimto so was given Ribena in any scenes that called for her to drink red wine. And Jim always makes sure there is apple juice in stock for Johnny Briggs, who prefers not to have to drink the burnt sugar mixture whenever Mike has a Scotch.

The props buyer orders fresh flowers and any food needed for the week ahead. Fresh vegetables and bread are ordered for the Corner Shop, pies and pasties and bacon and eggs are stocked up for Roy's Rolls, and any meals to be cooked in the characters' kitchens are also taken care of. The ingredients are bought in and quite often the set dressers will cook the food as required in a small kitchen at the back of studio – although they can't lay claim to Betty's famous

hot pot, which is ordered from the canteen and is quite popular with the cast. Any fresh food left over after a scene is thrown away, but the tins in the Corner Shop and the sweets in the Kabin aren't replaced nearly as frequently. A quick look on the shelves would probably reveal quite a few items past their sell-by dates!

Magazines have to be constantly renewed, though. Because *Coronation Street* is filmed three or four weeks before transmission it isn't possible to have the very latest issues on display, but they are kept as up to date as possible. We are constantly being sent magazines to put in the Kabin, covering every subject under the sun from fly fishing to fencing, but most of them are thrown away and the magazines you see on the shelves tend to be the general-interest weeklies and monthlies you would find in any shop. Newspapers are more tricky, and we have to make sure that there are never any time-sensitive headlines on display to spoil the illusion. Change is also supplied for the tills in the shops and pub, and any seasonal items such as Valentine's cards or Easter eggs also have to be stocked up on, just as they would in a real newsagent.

Despite the large amount of props kept in storage, there are always new things to find. After the design assistants have passed on the props list, the set dressers go through and tick off what they already have. Anything not in stock becomes the responsibility of props buyer John Eccles.

The props and furniture come from a variety of places. Some are bought, some hired – although for a long-term set it is obviously more cost-effective to buy an item. Until quite recently the same picture of David Powell from the Scout movement, which has hung in the hallway of No.1 since the mid 1980s, had been on hire for as

long as anyone remembered. Eventually a copy of it was made, and now *Coronation Street* pays a copyright fee each year and sends a fixed donation to the Scouts in return for its continued usage.

Viewers tend to be very observant about the props, so if a well-known ornament is smashed John will move heaven and earth to find a new one. 'It can be like looking for a needle in a haystack sometimes,' he sighs. Old favourites are always being mended and if you ever had the chance to look closely at the china props in *Coronation Street* you would see that a lot of them have been repeatedly glued together.

'Props do get smashed because it's in the nature of the job,' says Jim Coyle. 'The sets are always being moved in and out, and I've broken loads of things over the years. One night I remember dressing Ivy Tilsley's set and I picked up a box of small things, the contents of her china cabinet, and the bottom dropped out and everything shattered. I couldn't believe it!'

Things always tend to look better on screen, though, which can be a mixed blessing sometimes when you are striving for a downmarket look. 'I get letters from viewers asking where they can buy curtains and things and a lot of them I've picked up from flea markets or second-hand stalls,' says John. 'We try to dress *Coronation Street* down a little, but it's difficult because everything comes up looking good on camera, even things that are tatty in reality.'

Even so, John spends approximately £4000 a week on bits and pieces for the *Street*. Although there are always requirements for studio, a large part of the budget is spent on location props. Not all the sets can be built to order – and for many places that will only be seen briefly it makes sense to use an outside location. Naomi Ellwood is *Coronation Street*'s location manager and it is her job to find places suitable for filming, whether we are looking for houses, supermarkets, shops, offices or anywhere else the storylines take us. There are lots of practical and technical specifications when choosing a location set, but it must also be right from a design point of view – and this often means customizing a place to some extent.

Betty's famous hot pot.

Unmistakably
the Battersbys'.

There are usually three or four location sets each week, and once the style and period of the location is established Naomi will go out and photograph potential properties. I often prepare a brief beforehand, and sometimes I will get involved to the extent of specifying a particular look – for example, when we ran a storyline about a religious cult I wanted the house to look ordinary rather than eerie and made that clear from the outset.

When the location has been chosen a team will set out on a technical recce the Tuesday before filming begins. From the designer's point of view, this is the time to note down any changes that need to be made to the property and list any props they need to take along.

Occasionally the design department may decide to paint one wall of a house a different colour, change light fittings or put blinds up instead of curtains, and in this case the decorator will be sent out before the day of filming to make the alterations. Often, though, the changes are more superficial – adding pot plants and changing pictures or moving furniture. Whenever we make major alterations to a property the team are careful to take polaroid pictures of the way the room used to be and the decorator will be

sent back to return it to its original state when filming is over. Quite often, though, the owners are thrilled with the new look and are happy to keep it.

There are also practicalities to take care of. If we are filming at a church, hospital or business place, any signs showing their real name have to be covered up and replaced with ones bearing our fictional names of St Mary's Parish Church, Weatherfield General Hospital or Freshco. Some sets such as Freshco are regulars that have been dressed many times before, but many more are brand new and need careful thought and attention.

Sometimes a set which has been used on location will become increasingly important to the storyline, and at some point we will decide to build a replica set in studio. One example was Eunice's bed and breakfast, which began by making occasional appearances on screen but grew in importance as the weeks went on, with Jack and Vera eventually taking over the running of the establishment.

In these cases, because a room has already been seen by viewers, we have to make an authentic copy of the location house. This can be a daunting task, especially if the house hasn't been redecorated for some years and most of the ornaments and furnishings are

'I've broken loads of things over the years. One night I remember dressing Ivy Tilsley's set and I picked up a box of small things, the contents of her china cabinet, and the bottom dropped out and everything shattered. I couldn't believe it!'

discontinued lines. 'The turnover of stuff is phenomenal,' says John. 'Everyone remembers seeing things in the shops and says, "Oh, I know where you can get one of those." But they are probably thinking back over a couple of years and if they had to actually find the items today they'd be hard pressed to, even though they are still fresh in people's minds.'

Nevertheless, it is the team's challenge to do just that. Julian will take detailed photographs of a location from all angles, paste them up on a board and make lists of things to buy. Kitsch 1960s and 70s ornaments can be bought from flea markets and antique fairs, old televisions and hi-fis need to be resurrected from second-hand shops and wallpapers and materials have to be matched up to the originals. In the case of the B&B, the ornamental bar in the living room was so unique they had to have one specially made as there wasn't another to be found anywhere, but the rewards were worth it. 'We've had people pass comment on the set, saying it looks fabulous and that they remember going to guest houses like that,' says John. 'This job can be very satisfying when you manage to track things down and the sets start to take shape.'

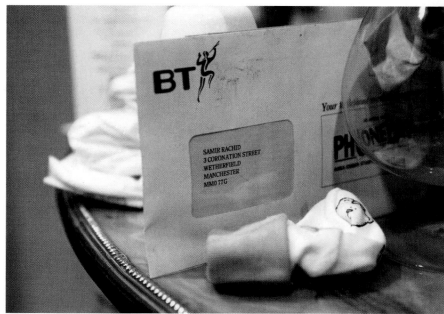

No detail is overlooked – even bills have to be carefully addressed before appearing on camera.

5

Behind
the
Scenes
Between
Scenes

The
Green Room

'*Coronation Street* has earned a unique place in the history of British television programme making. It is acknowledged as the best example of the craft of producing the television serial, written, directed and performed with speed, precision and excellence. It is screened across five continents and watched by over a hundred million people. It has never been out of the UK Top 10 since it was first networked in May 1961.'

This is the message that confronts the cast of *Coronation Street* as soon as they enter the Green Room. It is printed in imposing black letters above an artist's impression of the famous row of houses inside a huge picture frame. Hanging in the centre of one wall, it serves as a daily reminder of the programme's pedigree.

It is an awe-inspiring statement. But the actors and actresses who have become some of the most famous faces in Britain rarely have time to ponder the responsibility of appearing in the nation's

oldest and most successful programme. The pace generated by producing four episodes of quality television each week means that the Green Room is rarely still, although with up to 21 scenes being filmed in a single day the apparently chaotic epicentre is actually run with split-second precision.

The long days on *Coronation Street* usually start with make-up calls as early as 6.45am and rarely finish until 7.30pm, so it is essential that the cast have somewhere to relax on site during what can be

The Green Room in a rare quiet moment.

extremely long breaks between their scenes. The Green Room, which adjoins the studio where the interior sets are housed, provides that facility during the 51 weeks a year that the *Street* is in production.

For newcomers to the cast, and the occasional VIP guest, entering the Green Room is like walking into a strange parallel universe. At any one time you may see Ken Barlow reading the paper with a cup of coffee, Jim McDonald on the telephone organizing a charity cricket match and Maud Grimes impeccably dressed and minus her trademark wheelchair. And Steve McDonald, as manager of a virtual Manchester United, tapping a goal past Ashley Peacock's Inter Milan on the endlessly playing video game. After years of seeing the famous characters four times a week on television it can be disconcerting to see the cast gathered together in a place which resembles a slightly more opulent sixth-form common room.

'It's really weird when you walk in there for the first time because you think you know everyone but you don't,' says Naomi Radcliffe, who played Alison Wakefield. 'It's like putting on glasses that don't quite fit,' adds Jonathan Guy Lewis who played Sharon's treacherous fiancé Ian Bentley. 'You've seen everyone so many times before, and you have to keep reminding yourself that it's Barbara Knox rather than Rita Sullivan, and Liz Dawn rather than Vera Duckworth.'

Access to Stage One is strictly limited, and the Green Room in particular is very much regarded as the actors' own personal space. All visitors have to go through Stage One Security Lodge before being allowed into the building, and once that barrier is negotiated another security official, Alan Birch, is posted in a small reception immediately outside the doors to the studios and Green Room to deter any unfamiliar faces.

Invariably, there are problems with over-eager fans who will go to any lengths in order to meet their idols. Ex-policeman Alan concedes that there have been breaches of security in the past, especially with fans posing as extras or sneaking in from the adjacent Granada Studio Tours, but adds that most are easily dealt with.

'They just want to see the cast up close and ask for autographs, but you have to appreciate that this is a private area,' he explains. 'Even guests are frowned upon because this is somewhere where the cast go to learn lines or have a chat and a cup of tea somewhere out of the glare of publicity. As soon as they leave here to go home they are in the public eye again and this is somewhere where they can have a bit of peace.'

Not that the atmosphere is always tranquil. On busy days as many as 40 cast members can be present in the homely den filled with armchairs and plants, and decorated with framed photographs showing some of the highlights in the programme's 39-year history. Amongst a clutter of bags, coats and scripts, and accompanied by the soundtrack of a cacophony of mobile phones, some of the most famous men and women in Britain are gathered together as they wait to go on set.

Presiding over the chaos will be one of two rostered OSMs, or organizing stage managers. Each week the OSMs alternate roles, one working in studio directing the extras and the other 'on the desk' in the Green Room.

The desk job is unique in the world of television. No other programme has an equivalent position, which involves the not inconsiderable task of co-ordinating anything and everything to do with the artists. The OSM on desk must be manager, agent and agony aunt to the actors, as well as fulfilling their primary role of making sure that everybody arrives in studio on time for their scenes.

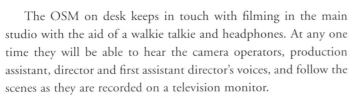

The OSM on desk keeps in touch with filming in the main studio with the aid of a walkie talkie and headphones. At any one time they will be able to hear the camera operators, production assistant, director and first assistant director's voices, and follow the scenes as they are recorded on a television monitor.

Guided by a printed scene-by-scene schedule, they must ensure that everyone arrives on time and smooth out unexpected crises such as artists arriving late after getting stuck in traffic, or scenes being brought forward from the following day. They must also deal with every problem imaginable, from finding lost scripts to ensuring a ready supply of tea, coffee and biscuits has been delivered from the catering department. Add to this a constantly ringing desk phone, and the pressure really starts to mount up.

As well as the principal artists, crew and extras, the OSM on desk also has to deal with all the other offices connected to *Coronation Street*. On a typical day the OSM liaises with people from artists' payments, casting, the production office and the press office, as well as taking messages from the cast's agents, friends and family.

'A lot of people rely on us and we have to function as a kind of information desk,' confirms OSM Freddy Carpen-Jukes. 'If someone asks something and we don't know we have to be able to find out quickly, and it can get quite nerve-racking. You need a sense of humour to do this job, and you need to be able to take things lightly, because everyone gets stressed sometimes and if you took any remarks that occasionally come your way, good or bad, to heart, then you wouldn't be able to carry on.'

The day-to-day atmosphere varies according to which artists are in studio. When the younger actors predominate you can guarantee that a general air of madness will prevail and on blocking days, when the whole cast for the week are assembled to run through the scenes

for timings and camera positions, there can be pandemonium.

'Blocking days are definitely the hardest because it's the first day of the week when they all see each other and they want to catch up on the gossip,' says Freddy. 'You have to prise them out of the Green Room and into the studio because they are all deep in conversation. Sometimes it's so mad that you just want to shout "Be quiet!" but it's great because they all have a great sense of humour and you hear some very funny things.'

The *Coronation Street* cast is often described as one big happy family, and while this is a cliché, the artists do all get along together – something which is essential as they spend so much time in each other's company. And as with any workplace, some deep and lasting friendships are formed, with several of the younger actors sharing city-centre flats off screen and socializing together in the evenings.

Team spirit is taken to its logical conclusion with the *Coronation Street* football and cricket teams – testaments to whose victories festoon every available ledge in the Green Room in the form of various trophies, which stand side by side with the programme's many accolades from the television industry.

In summer cricket is the hot topic in the Green Room. Charles Lawson captains the *Coronation Street* XI, a team variously consisting of Sean Wilson, Mike Le Vell, Steven Arnold, Simon Gregson, Kevin Kennedy, Chris Bisson, Tom Wisdom, Ian Mercer and old boy Nick Cochrane, as well as some supplementary players from the production team and press office. The female cast members from Tracy Shaw to Elizabeth Bradley are enthusiastic fans, accompanying the team to games to cheer them on.

Most matches are with local clubs or businesses and always draw a crowd, but the athletic actors have also batted and bowled in testimonial matches for county players such as Mike Watkinson,

Top: A deserted
Green Room.
Bottom: Signed
photographs for fans.

Steve Rhodes and Richard Illingworth. During the 1998 season the team were staggeringly successful and enjoyed victory in most games. 'It's a lot of fun,' says Kevin Kennedy. 'We have a laugh and raise money for charity. We don't always have time to go out in a group unless it's for an official function, and it's brilliant the way everyone pulls together. We may not be test cricketers or even county cricketers but we more than hold our own.'

The football team are less active, but *Coronation Street* actors including Mike Le Vell, Simon Gregson and Sean Wilson have been known to join forces with actors from *Brookside* and a few ex-professionals for occasional matches, and play to quite a high standard. Although not a sportsman himself, Bill Tarmey is the 'non-practical' coach for these games. He may not actually lead the team in training, but according to ex-team member Phil Middlemiss, he does make sure he takes everybody out for a drink afterwards.

As well as the sporting trophies, there are other clues to some of the cast's off-screen activities nestling amongst the running schedules, script amendments and holiday lists on the Green Room noticeboards. The *Coronation Street* artists are in constant demand from charities and the two pinboards groan under the weight of invitations to charity balls, and requests to open local functions or attend fundraising evenings. Although there are far too many demands on the cast's time for them to be able to attend each one, most have their own favourites and support them as much as possible.

While general requests are posted on the packed noticeboards, many more take the form of personal letters to individuals. Letters and packages addressed to the cast are taken to the Green Room twice daily, and then posted in a huge wooden rack of pigeonholes near the front door. Established cast members of more than a few months have their own pigeonhole, while new or short-term cast members can look for their name in three general boxes labelled A - H, I - O and P - Z, situated above the letterboxes for costume, make-up, design and props.

One thing that all the pigeonholes have in common, though, is that they are constantly packed to the seams. If an actor is on

holiday for a few weeks, his or her letters are often forwarded to his or her home as the sheer volume of mail is overwhelming and cannot be contained in the 5" x 10" slots.

It would take each actor a full working week every week to reply individually to all the letters, so some of the less personal correspondence and requests for signed photographs are dealt with by security man Alan Birch.

'**You have to prise them out of the Green Room and into the studio because they are all deep in conversation. Sometimes it's so mad that you just want to shout "Be quiet!" but it's great because they all have a great sense of humour and you hear some very funny things.**'

onerous task, and many of the actors like to retreat from the hubbub of the Green Room to the privacy of their own dressing rooms to catch up with letter writing and learn their scripts.

The compact but comfortable dressing rooms fill three floors of corridors adjacent to the studio and are arranged in order of longevity of service. William Roache and Eileen Derbyshire are on the ground floor right next to the studio entrance, and newer cast members occupy the top dressing rooms two floors up. The newest cast members of all, or those on a short-term contract, are allocated one of the spare dressing rooms on a weekly basis, which they may or may not have to share. Finally being given a room of their own with a nameplate on the door is a gratifying moment and a symbol of establishment for most *Coronation Street* actors.

The windowless rooms all have approximately the same basic décor of plain walls and carpet, and each one is supplied with a wardrobe, one upright and one comfortable chair and a dressing table with a centrally placed, well-lit mirror. Many artists, though, especially those less keen on the constant chaos downstairs, have gone to great lengths to personalise their private retreats. Many of the cluttered dens are virtual homes from home, containing televisions, fridges, bookshelves and ornaments, and displaying

'Big stars like Liz Dawn get literally hundreds of letters every day and they could never get through them all, so they will sign photographs and I send them off on their behalf,' affirms Alan. 'When a new person starts they have a huge influx of mail and then it levels off, but the young lads like Steven Arnold still get sackfuls of letters from girl fans even after a couple of years.'

Even with Alan's help, answering all the fan mail can be an

'When a new person starts they have a huge influx of mail and then it levels off, but the young lads still get sackfuls of letters from girl fans even after a couple of years.'

colourful photographs of family and friends on the walls.

Amanda Barrie's retreat is furnished with antique tables, rugs, cushions and a wooden artist's model that reflects her love of drawing and painting. She spends hours in her room reading *The Sporting Life*, watching the horse racing and making endless calls on her mobile phone.

Bill Roache often misses breakfast and keeps Frosties and Ryvitas in his room which is cluttered with letters, pens, papers and a stack of books on alternative religions. He also keeps a replica of one of Uncle Albert's pot dogs, crafted for him out of orange soap by an art student, and a portable radio so that he can listen to cricket test matches.

Betty Driver likes to do tapestry to calm down and de-stress in a cosy boudoir filled with photographs and new-age crystals, and Liz Dawn has invested in a huge armchair so she can have a snooze whenever she likes. But other dressing rooms, notably those belonging to the more gregarious young male cast members, are

almost bare and it is obvious that they are only ever used for hasty costume changes between scenes.

The dressers from the wardrobe department are amongst the few people to be allowed into the cast's dressing rooms, being equipped with keys in order to leave character costumes for the actors to change into, either for scenes or for publicity photoshoots. Another person with unlimited access is Bea, *Coronation Street*'s dedicated cleaner, who keeps both the Green Room and the dressing rooms spotless.

The cast implicitly trusts Bea, who has worked for Granada for many years, and they repay her loyalty with great affection. Transformed by the make-up and costume departments to look like Joan Collins, she was even chosen as the guest of honour when cast members led by Denise Welch and Vicky Entwistle held an unofficial champagne opening of the new third-floor dressing rooms in 1998.

As well as the principal artists, Stage One is home to the many extras or background artists – the unsung heroes and heroines of every Rovers, cafe and location scene. Varying numbers of men and women aged between 18 and 87 are used each day, and they have their own rooms – one for men and one for women – at the far end of the upper floor corridors. Although they rarely have to deliver any lines, their days are often as long as those of the principals, but many of the extras have worked together for years and the atmosphere is one of friendly camaraderie.

The youngest *Street* stars are also housed in the Stage One complex. The children's room is a bright and airy place, painted yellow with a huge round window looking out on to an ornamental garden and Granada Breeze studios. It is a Green Room in miniature with tiny red plastic chairs instead of the blue and maroon armchairs of the main quarters, brightly coloured child-size tables, a television and a huge box of games and cuddly toys. Here the children – from tiny babies Lewis Ablett and Megan Foster who play the Mallet twins, to 16-year-old cast members – sit with their chaperones waiting to be called on set.

The children aren't allowed to neglect their education, though. Until they reach the legal school-leaving age Granada are bound by law to employ a tutor to ensure that they don't fall behind in their lessons. In many ways it is an exceptional educational opportunity as they are offered one-to-one attention which isn't widely available in schools, but it can be difficult for them to concentrate with so much going on.

Another communal area is the smokers' room to the rear of the building. Stage One has a general no-smoking policy, but a room is provided for those who wish to indulge. Like the rest of the building, the yellow room has a television, armchairs and tables, although it is sparser than the main Green Room and lacks the personal touches of pictures and noticeboards.

The cast also have access to a small kitchen off the Green Room, where tea and coffee machines continually dispense drinks into polystyrene cups, boxes of biscuits, Ryvitas and bowls of fruit are laid out for between-scene snacking, and a fridge is filled with milk, yoghurts, cheese and butter. With so many long breaks in the day, it can be tempting to graze constantly to pass the time. But the figure conscious can avoid temptation by going to a nearby gym – always keeping their mobile phones handy in case they are called back for a sooner than expected scene.

For maximum speed and convenience, lunch – a choice of hot meals or healthy salads – is served on site at Granada during the week. On the days when filming is outdoors a catering wagon is

parked in the grounds of Stage One. And on studio days Granada facilities provide food in the restaurant of the main building a few hundred yards away. When Studio Tours is open, lucky customers on the street may catch a glimpse of their favourite actors as they go to lunch, often escorted by Alan Birch, who will drive people the short distance in inclement weather to protect their make-up and costumes.

Lunch is usually between 1.00pm and 2.00pm – so for those involved in the final scenes of the day there are still five or six working hours to go. In the winter months, actors – and certainly crew – get up in the dark and drive home in the dark, so time spent in Stage One makes up an overwhelming part of their lives. It is a unique little community with a unique atmosphere – exciting, frenetic and unpredictable. But whatever difficulties the day brings, those who work there consistently pull together to produce the most popular programme on television.

Amanda Barrie and Johnny Briggs go over their lines.

6

Coronation

Street

in the

Studio

Filming on Set

For most people the concept of television production conjures up a popular image of studio filming, as witnessed in many 'behind the scenes' documentaries or dramatizations about the industry. They picture a busy, exciting environment where the artists deliver their lines and are captured on camera, with a team of directors, assistants and technical staff on hand to ensure that everything goes smoothly. But few people realize the sheer precision and planning involved, nor do they appreciate that the week in studio makes up less than a quarter of the overall schedule.

At any one time on *Coronation Street* there are four separate directors, working at different stages of production. A lot of initial preparation has to be put in before they are ready to start filming, and as ever the starting point is the script.

A director will receive copies of their scripts three or four weeks before filming begins, at which point we have a meeting to discuss the episodes. This often takes hours and can be very specific. *Coronation Street* employs several different directors, and each has their own way of working. When a new director comes on board, we literally go through the scripts together page by page, but once I know someone's work and have built up a relationship with them, then the process can be shortened.

Thu, Apr 8, 1999	**Coronation Street.Wk.15 Eps.604-607**	Page 7
	DRAFT SCHEDULE	

SCENE(S)	I/E	SET DESCRIPTION	D/N	PAGES

4604/15   INT   ROVERS BAR   DAY 1–1930   4 3/8
Page 48–5   *Eunice plans tea for 2, Spider asks Curly for advice, Alison miffed because her and Kevin are never alone*
Screen Time:

CURLY WATTS	KEVIN KENNEDY
JACK DUCKWORTH	BILL TARMEY
KEVIN WEBSTER	MICHAEL LE VELL
SPIDER/GEOFFREY	MARTIN HANCOCK
VERA DUCKWORTH	LIZ DAWN
ALISON WAKEFIELD	NAOMI RADCLIFFE
EUNICE GEE	MEG JOHNSON

Coronation St. regulars.

4605/2   INT   ASHLEY'S LIVING ROOM   DAY 2–0930   2 1/8
Page 4–6   *Ashley gives Leanne the third degree about last night*
Screen Time:

ASHLEY PEACOCK	STEVEN ARNOLD
LEANNE BATTERSBY	JANE DANSON

aspirin in cupboard, dress kitchen cupboards, prac water

4605/14   INT   ASHLEY'S LIVING ROOM   DAY 2–1815   2 1/8
Page 46–4   *Vikram tells Leanne he can't take her out*
Screen Time:

ASHLEY PEACOCK	STEVEN ARNOLD
LEANNE BATTERSBY	JANE DANSON
VIKRAM DESAI	CHRIS BISSON

nail varnish

4605/8   INT   ROVERS BAR   DAY 2–1430   4 4/8
Page 25–2   *Vikram gets dragged away by his dad, Deirdre queries and invoice with Mike and Gary's got the job at Eunice's*
Screen Time:

ALMA BALDWIN	AMANDA BARRIE
DEIRDRE RACHID	ANNE KIRKBRIDE
GARY MALLETT	IAN MERCER
JACK DUCKWORTH	BILL TARMEY
LEANNE BATTERSBY	JANE DANSON
MIKE BALDWIN	JOHNNY BRIGGS
RAVI DESAI	SAEED JAFFREY
VIKRAM DESAI	CHRIS BISSON

Coronation St. regulars.

4605/16   INT   ROVERS BAR   DAY 2–1830   5 2/8
Page 52–5   *Jack has not turned up, leanne is going out with Tom, Audrey is not pleased*
Screen Time:

AUDREY ROBERTS	SUE NICHOLLS
JIM MCDONALD	CHARLES LAWSON
JUDY MALLETT	GAYNOR FAYE
KEVIN WEBSTER	MICHAEL LE VELL
LEANNE BATTERSBY	JANE DANSON
SALLY WEBSTER	SALLY WHITTAKER
VERA DUCKWORTH	LIZ DAWN
DANNY HARGREAVES	RICHARD STANDING
TOM FERGUSON	TOM WISDOM

Coronation St. regulars.

A filming schedule.

Directing *Coronation Street* is a demanding job. Because we have such a large and varied cast, a director must be able to manage people properly and have good communication skills as well as understanding the scripts. They need to look after the artists and make sure their performances are spot on, while simultaneously possessing all the technical skills necessary to shoot four scripts a week on multi-camera without panicking under pressure.

By now the buff first-draft scripts have been transformed into pink second-draft scripts and are almost finalized. These are the floor copies that are distributed to the crew. Any dialogue changes should already have been made at this point, so by the time I sit down with the director we are discussing the scripts in terms of mood, performance and continuity. After this meeting I probably won't see them again until they begin shooting, and although the lines of communication are always open it is essential that I convey my ideas to them fully at this stage.

For example, I may have asked for a scene to be rewritten to make it less violent during a script-editing meeting, but if it is still on the aggressive side, it can be modified by careful direction, taking out some of the physical action.

Because the directors arrive at the story at a set point and haven't seen the previous or future scripts, it is my job to provide an overall picture. As the producer it is up to me to indicate when a particular scene performs an important plot function. So if a little white lie in one script is going to have repercussions six weeks down the line, I will point out that it needs special emphasis.

Any amendments arising from this meeting are given to the PA/script supervisor, who makes a final check of the pink scripts before producing the white rehearsal scripts. These are the definitive article, and are distributed to the cast approximately a week before they begin filming. Separate day-by-day scripts are also distributed to those involved in scenes on location.

After our meeting, the director has various tasks to address. They must help cast any characters that are to make a first appearance in their episodes – and this often means auditioning several new faces. Next, they must speak to the production designer about any special requirements they have for the week, as well as attending recces to determine new locations.

When this stage of the preparation has been completed, the director works on the camera scripts. These are detailed visual interpretations of the rehearsal scripts, upon which all the camera shots are marked down for the benefit of the crew and, later on, the vision editor. There are three cameras operating in studio, which are vision mixed as recording occurs. The director draws lines to illustrate how and where he wants shots to be cut, and by the time the crew get into studio, each script has been broken down into approximately 400 different camera shots. Now that *Coronation Street* records four episodes a week there is little time for rehearsal, so it is necessary to mentally co-ordinate and choreograph the camera and artists' moves beforehand.

A rostered director will have two key team members working with them on a block – the production assistant and first assistant director. Both have different but complementary roles and work very closely with the director to facilitate their schedules and ensure

that everything is running smoothly.

While the director is working on his scripts with a view to plotting camera shots, the PA is simultaneously going through them to ensure each episode is the right length – 24 minutes, which includes one minute and 42 seconds for the titles and sponsorship credits. They read through the dialogue and use a stop watch to note down the timings for each scene.

'I read them out loud to myself and try to match the style of the actress or actor,' says Tina Kirk, one of the regular PAs. 'Some characters talk very quickly, like the Battersbys who are always rowing, but others like Fred Elliott talk very slowly and elaborate a lot. I also allow time for the actions, so if someone knocks on the door in a scene I account for that as well.

'After a while you can actually tell whether you are going to be over or under just by holding a script in your hand,' she adds. 'If a script is 70 pages or less it might well be under. Sometimes, though, you get lots of emotional scenes which just spread and spread, so it does vary.'

Once the scenes have been roughly timed, the totals are added up and a timesheet is produced for myself, the script editor and the

director. From this we can see whether the episode is likely to be too long or too short, and therefore whether we need to make cuts or ask for an extra scene to be written. Timing is crucial to television drama as we are not allowed more than 30 seconds leeway in either direction, and these checks are repeated again and again throughout blocking and filming.

The PA also prepares a synopsis of each scene that goes at the front of the rehearsal script, and a character crossblock. This useful document is forwarded to the make-up and wardrobe departments and functions as an 'at a glance guide' to which artists are in which scenes.

Meanwhile, the first assistant director has been busy working from the pink scripts to prepare a schedule for the week. Just as television pictures are fragmented and reassembled during transmission, *Coronation Street* is shot out of sequence, and the scenes are numbered and arranged in order again during editing.

There are many factors to be taken into account while preparing a schedule. Initially, any scenes to be shot on location need to be separated from the studio scenes. Location filming normally begins on Sunday, continuing on Monday and often

running into Tuesday as well, with Wednesday, Thursday and Friday being the days when the studio scenes are shot.

The first guesses approximately how long each scene will take to complete. A lot can depend on which cast and crew members are around that week, and understanding how everyone works takes time and experience. Each director has slightly different methods and takes varying amounts of time to shoot an episode, just as some actors cope better with heavy storylines and having to memorize one long scene after another. For actors who have a tremendous amount of emotional scenes over several episodes, a first may try to arrange their scenes in story order to make things easier for them. Or they may want to spread the character's scenes evenly over several days to allow them chance to learn all their lines. A practised first can estimate how long each scene will take to film and put down provisional timings, which a director may amend as they decide specifically how they intend to shoot them.

As well as making sure the schedule works from an actor's and director's point of view, there are any number of special considerations which the first has to take into account. 'It can be very limiting when the children are in because they can only work

between 9.30am and 4.00pm, preferably in the afternoons, so if there's a storyline with the Webster or Platt children you are snookered by restrictions,' says Dayle Evans. 'Press commitments such as awards ceremonies and photo-shoots can also cause problems. Artists may need to be released for a day or an afternoon, and all their scenes must then be fitted in around that.'

On very busy weeks it can be impossible to fit all the scenes into the schedule, and a pre-shoot may be called for, where several scenes are shot the week before. While this eases the agenda for the week ahead, it can also prove difficult to organize if the artists involved feature in the previous week's block. Their availability for the pre-shoot therefore depends on the goodwill of the preceding director and first, who will have to alter their schedule in order to accommodate it.

There can also be the hassle of last-minute alterations. 'It's constantly changing,' says Dayle. 'Perhaps an artist will become ill and there will be rewrites, and you'll have to cope with that. Some weeks you might get a call late on Friday afternoon of the previous week saying that someone is ill, so you have to reschedule which can be a nightmare.' Every alteration seems to have repercussions and organizing the schedule is a carefully balanced juggling act.

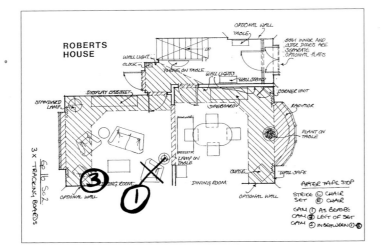

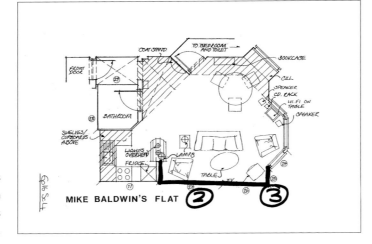

Floor plans with camera positions numbered.

When the director has finished camera scripting, and the first has completed the schedule, the PA inputs all this information into the computer. The camera scripts are typed up in episode order, and the camera shots and shot numbers are put in. Only twenty of these are printed, and they are distributed to a few key people – the director, vision mixer, boom operators, senior sound, lighting director, organizing stage managers and first. The three camera operators approach the scenes from a purely visual point of view, and are given camera cards, which the PA also prints out. These don't include the scenes' dialogue, but simply have the shot numbers on the left and shot descriptions on the right-hand sides.

With the numerous preparations completed, it's time to begin filming. After the location scenes are filmed there is a blocking session which takes place prior to shooting in studio. This usually

happens on a Tuesday. The director, all the artists, camera crew leader, lighting director, senior sound, charge hand, designer, action props, OSMs and first assistant director all attend this session where the scenes for the rest of the week are run through, moves jotted down and any technical points made. Sometimes the writers of these episodes will also attend, which can be useful as they can check that their lines have been correctly interpreted and, if not, have a timely word with the director.

However, the block is not a rehearsal for the actors as such. Instead, the main focus of concentration is on the actual mechanics of a scene. It deals with the physical, rather than emotional details, so actors will be told when to sit or stand, when to cross the room and when to stay still. This is the one chance for everyone involved to see what the action consists of before filming begins.

The scenes for the next four episodes are run through in story order, excluding any scenes to be shot on location. The first announces the scene number and where it is to take place, and the whole crew march from one set to another, furiously making notes as they go along.

The first and OSM have copies of the scripts with them, as do the actors – many of whom are still reading from them at this stage as there is a little time left to learn the scenes properly later in the week.

The other departments carry a set of floor plans. Two lots of copies are produced – one in story order, which is how the block is done, and one in schedule order which is the order in which the scenes will actually be filmed later in the week.

Each page of the floor plan gives an episode number, scene number and location, complete with a detailed technical drawing of that set and its various props. Upon these are marked the positions of cameras 1, 2 and 3, and any additional information such as when a tape stop will occur. This is when the cameras stop rolling to allow for changes in camera positions, and perhaps for a reset. The Rovers Return scenes tend to be the most complicated, as they are longer and feature several different groups of people in the same room. Just one Rovers scene may involve changing camera

'Sometimes they will virtually take a set to pieces just to get one shot, and then have to put it all back together again.'

positions three or four times, jumping from alcove to alcove and taking out various walls or booths in order to accommodate these moves. 'Sometimes they will virtually take a set to pieces just to get one shot, and then have to put it all back together again,' observes props man Jim Coyle.

While the director is talking the artist through their moves, everyone else is anticipating how this will affect them. A seemingly innocuous action can involve several departments' co-operation to ensure that things go smoothly. For example, if Gail were to fill a kettle and switch it on, the props department would have to make sure that there was water available when the taps were turned on. And that there was an electricity socket on the wall for the kettle to be plugged into, and that it worked. There are working taps situated every 20 feet around the studio, although they only supply cold water. On the day, the plumbers simply add back hoses to the sinks and attach them to the taps. Most of the plug sockets also work, although some are dummies, and the props department book an electrician to come and wire them up if the script calls for it.

If Gail also had to cross the room before putting the kettle on, the sound department would have to decide if the move could be covered by one microphone or if another would be necessary, and how many poles and booms to use. The camera crew leader needs to note down which direction they will be shooting in, and the lighting department would have to check that everything was organized at their end too, deciding which areas of the set need to be lit. They would also have to look out for any lighting changes such as characters turning lights on or off, and check the fictional time of day of the scene, which would affect the light outside a window.

The block usually takes a couple of hours. Further small cuts will be made at this stage, to ensure an episode is running to time. The first or OSM makes sure that any important notes are passed on to the cast and crew and to departments not attending the block such as make-up and wardrobe. Then, after the block, it is time for rehearsals.

Before *Coronation Street* produced four episodes a week, it was

The studio
lighting gallery.

possible to rehearse each and every scene beforehand. Now, with the busy schedules, not everything fits into the available rehearsal time. For this reason, only the most challenging scenes are selected. The director looks over the scripts and decides which scenes will need work, then a schedule is drawn up and distributed. 'The director will usually pick out the demanding emotional scenes for a rehearsal,' says PA Wendy Rollason. 'Also, he will check to see if there are any new artists beginning that week, and try to give them a rehearsal to break them in gently.'

Unlike the block, the rehearsals concentrate on the emotional nuances of a scene. This is the last chance for an artist to perfect their performance before the actual filming days, when time in studio is very tight and a professional, word-perfect rendering of the script is expected. Despite the pressure of producing 96 minutes of drama a week – the equivalent of many feature films – *Coronation Street* consistently strives to maintain, and even improve upon, the quality of the programme, and we are fortunate in having such a talented and committed cast to help us achieve that goal.

On Wednesday morning studio filming begins. By this point the first assistant director will have worked out how many background artists are needed each day, and the booking assistant will have arranged for them to come in. The background artists aren't needed for blocking or rehearsals and are only brought in for filming. Even then, they only come on set for a take, as do babies Lewis Ablett and Megan Foster who play the Mallet twins. The babies become weary spending a lot of time on set and are replaced with plastic dolls until the cameras are ready to roll.

The PA will have ordered any additional material required – for example, if the characters are watching television and the screen is in shot, they must order a VHS tape of a programme and clear it with the rights department, even if it is only to be seen for a second. *Coronation Street* usually sticks to Granada's own productions to simplify the process, with quiz shows and documentaries being favourites. Meanwhile, the OSM on the

studio floor will have read the scripts and made notes, and let the artists know of any last-minute dialogue changes.

Filming starts at 8.15am and continues until 7.15pm with an hour for lunch and two tea breaks. The days are longer for many of the crew, and the artists in the first scenes of the day have to be in earlier for their make-up calls.

Each cast and crew member has a call sheet and a schedule, typed up and distributed by the production secretary. These give brief details of each scene in filming order, including the scene and episode numbers, place, fictional time, characters involved, page numbers on scripts and estimated time on screen, as well as brief details of the action and notes for props.

With everything prepared, it is time to commit the studio scenes to camera, and we have just three days to record them. *Coronation Street* operates on a rehearse/record basis. Each scene is run through two or three times, and when everybody is happy the director will go for a take. I watch proceedings in studio on a television monitor in my office, and can phone downstairs if I want to make any changes.

Generally speaking, the director will work from the production control room, or box, although some prefer to direct from the studio floor. The first assistant director, cameramen, boom operators, OSMs and lighting gaffer are all on talkback, and wear headphones which allow them to hear instructions from the box – which is actually three booths, arranged side by side. Most departments can only hear instructions relevant to them, but the firsts can hear everybody and cut in on any conversation.

In the middle box, watching the action on a monitor, are the director, PA and vision mixer. The vision mixer sits in front of three screens, each showing the point of view of one of the cameras, and alternates between them as the PA calls the shots announcing the number of the next shot and which camera it is going to be on. To the right-hand side of the director's box is the sound desk, which is louder than anywhere else in studio and boasts an impressive-looking sound console with myriad buttons controlling all the

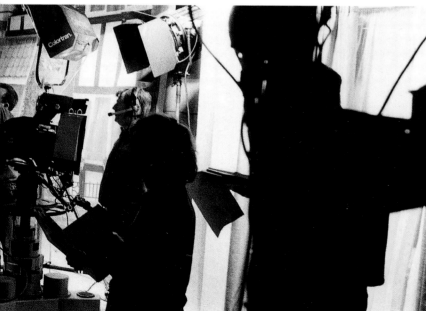

Liz Dawn and Bill
Tarmey enjoy a joke
with first assistant
director John Friend
Newman.

studio microphones. On the left-hand side is the lighting director
and console operator, the vision engineer who looks after the
cameras technically and monitors the picture quality, and the VT
recorder who actually rolls the tape.

Out on the floor are the camera operators and lighting crew,
make-up and wardrobe, the grips who carry and assemble all the
equipment, lay cables and put down tracking for the cameras, and
the stage hands who move the scenery in and out. Action props are
a constant presence on the set, ready to step in to refill glasses in the
Rovers, move props around and generally have anything and
everything required for the scene to hand. A director will be very
specific about how he wants the set to look on screen and
everything must be in exactly the right place. The organizing stage
manager is on the floor at all times, liaising with the OSM on desk
to make sure that the actors for the next scene are always standing
by ready. The OSM also positions and directs the background
artists, suggesting actions to them and dashing to and from the
monitors to make sure they are in the right place and that there are
no holes in the picture.

The OSM also helps the first assistant director, whose job it is
to be the director's voice on set, effectively conveying their wishes
to the assembled team. It is up to the first to set the pace for the
day – which is necessarily quite a fast one. 'You go in there and
you are racing against the clock from the minute you start until
the minute you finish on a Friday evening. You are the one who
makes it happen for the director, the one who knows the speed
you have to go at, and you have to push to keep everyone moving
and on schedule,' says Dayle. 'If the director starts to fall behind
it's up to you to say, "We're running out of time," and suggest
going for a take.'

Deciding when to go for a take is far more complicated than
most people imagine. It isn't merely a question of waiting until the
director is happy with what the actors are doing, although this is a
large part of it. Every department has to be satisfied that the scene
is working for them. Because of the preparation done during

'I think every director should do this programme.'

blocking, the technical details should be worked out, but there are always little adjustments to be made on the day. Lighting and cameras have to be just right, and sound have to make sure there are no problems with the microphones, and that the poles aren't casting shadows on the actors, because the lighting is in the same place. So the rehearsal time is as much about ironing out any practical problems as it is about perfecting the artists' performances.

It is incredibly difficult to keep to a strict time schedule. Often a scene that looks quite short on paper will take over an hour because the director wants to shoot it from several angles. Then again, a long scene in terms of dialogue may go very smoothly and take less time than expected. Odd things can cause problems. A character wearing a noisy plastic mac could mean difficulties for the sound crew. Or the lighting department may need time to sort out a problem with flaring on a particular surface. At any one point in the day we can be very far ahead, or trailing behind, but somehow it all evens itself out, and every scene always gets finished by Friday evening.

When all departments are satisfied, the director will call for a take, and convey this to the first via headphones. The first will order everyone to stand by, and make-up and costume will come and do their final checks on the artists. Then the first sees that everyone is ready to go on the floor and the director has stopped talking to the cameras, and announces that they are going for a take. When the PA hears this she asks the vision operator to roll to record. She then counts down from ten seconds, which the first can hear via headphones. On zero, the first shouts 'Action', and filming begins.

There may be several takes before everyone is happy, and the PA notes down each of these with details of the different shots, marking the one which the director decides is best. When the final take has been played back on the monitors and checked, the team move straight on to the next scene.

Throughout the day, the PA times each take, listening out for any glitches in the script and keeping a careful eye on continuity. No detail is too tiny to be picked up on by the PA. If an actor is wearing their own watch and the time displayed isn't the same as the time of the scene, the PA will spot it. They notice every little thing, from which shoulder someone is carrying their bag over to whether they were holding a drink in their right or left hand, and they make notes throughout.

At the end of the day, the PA will write up a continuity report sheet with the date, director, PA and all the information about the day's filming. She will write down which scenes have been completed, how much cut film has been shot, whether they have dropped any scenes or added any extra and how long the episode is currently running at. I receive a copy of this document on a day-to-day basis, and if I see we are under-running I might suggest an extra scene. The writer then has to turn it around very quickly and tailor it to whichever artists are available the next day and which sets are up in studio.

Filming is not an exact science, and in theory a director could go on shooting a scene for ever to get that perfect take. But in order to achieve our target of four programmes a week, an important part of the job is knowing when to stop. 'I think every director should do this programme,' says Michael Kerrigan, who has directed a wide range of drama from *Dr Who* to the acclaimed production of *The Phoenix and the Carpet,* and who won an Emmy for his work on Jim Henson's *Mother Goose Stories.* 'It's such good discipline. You have to work as a team on *Coronation Street* – there's no point in saying,"I want to do this. It's going to take an hour but I have to have it." We must hit the schedule, or else it is irresponsible. But the crew are very professional here. They get on with the job, and there's still enough room for a director and his team to work well and put their mark on it. It's bloody hard work, but it's very fulfilling.'

7

Coronation Street
on **PSC**

Filming on Location

One of the main factors contributing to *Coronation Street*'s phenomenal success is the old-fashioned sense of community for which the programme has always been applauded. Life in Weatherfield centres around the local pub and shops, the residents all know and care about each other, and everybody seems to know everyone else's business.

These days such close-knit neighbourhoods are increasingly rare and the relatively cloistered society of *Coronation Street* invokes nostalgia and affection in the minds of the viewers. In order to maintain the community feeling, it is important that the street itself remains the main star of the programme, and so the majority of the action still tends to take place in the terraced homes and back-street businesses that audiences have known and loved for years.

There are also practical reasons for this. Filming on PSC (another term for location filming referring to the initials of the portable single camera used to film outside studio) takes much longer than filming on multi-camera, and it would prove impossible to produce four programmes a week if there were an over-emphasis on location scenes.

Nevertheless, *Coronation Street* would be completely unrealistic in the late twentieth century if its characters confined themselves entirely to their immediate surroundings, and there are frequently occasions when the scripts necessitate filming further afield.

Despite the proliferation of local businesses on the street – with Underworld, the salon, the pub and two shops providing employment for a large percentage of Weatherfield, and Roy's Rolls

just around the corner on Victoria Street – the unlucky residents who haven't found jobs on their immediate doorsteps have to pursue careers elsewhere. Freshco and the open-air market are the two main sources of work.

Special occasions also require separate locations. Weddings, christenings and funerals all demand churches or registry offices, then there are hotels, nightclubs and wine bars for when the social animals of the street branch out from the restrictions of the Rovers. Meanwhile, anyone falling ill is taken to Weatherfield General, where Martin Platt works as a nurse.

Regulars not residing on *Coronation Street* need to be found flats or houses if they are to be seen at home. And there are numerous other locations to be sought out, including streets, parks, doctors', offices, police stations and any of the other places the characters might conceivably visit from time to time.

It is the job of location manager Naomi Ellwood to find potential places and arrange for us to film there. Four weeks before filming she will break down the buff scripts, making a note of anywhere new that is mentioned. Typically there will be three or four supplementary locations a week, as well as filming on the lot,

the purpose-built outdoor street set.

Working with four separate directors at different stages in their schedules means that Naomi will have several locations to bear in mind at any one time. 'If it's straightforward I will leave it until a couple of weeks before filming begins, but if there is somewhere more difficult I start the search earlier,' she says. Some locations such as Frescho are used regularly, so it is just a case of arranging a mutually convenient time to film with the host supermarket. Others, however, have to be set up from scratch.

The location manager goes out and compiles a shortlist for each site, using their knowledge of the local area. So if we are looking to film in a pub, for example, Naomi discusses the style and period of the place with the director and designer and then takes photographs of three or four buildings that meet their

specifications. From the pictures, they narrow the choice down to one or two before going out to take a closer look.

If the director decides from the initial recce that it has what they need for the scene, Naomi will approach whoever owns the pub, arrange a fee with them and draw up a location agreement, which has to be signed before filming can begin. This is a contract between Granada Television and the location owner confirming the dates and hours of filming. Granada also issues locations with a copy of our public liability insurance in case anyone is hurt on the premises.

Some locations are more specific than others, so these take priority during the initial trawl. 'If we were looking for a jewellers, for example, there are only so many in and around Manchester, so I would find that location first,' explains Naomi. 'Then, because the schedule is so tight, I would work outwards on a radius from

strong crew into a quiet cul-de-sac without causing a huge amount of disruption, so as a matter of courtesy we like to warn residents before our arrival. On the whole, most people are fine about us filming, and usually like to stay and watch, which isn't a problem as long as they remain quiet during a take.

With larger locations, especially working environments, there is a different set of obstacles to face. Hospitals can be especially tricky, and one option is to find a disused one to film in. Another solution is for the location manager to work closely with the first assistant director and schedule filming for a time when it will be quiet and there aren't any visitors. Sometimes we can arrange to film on a Sunday in a part of the hospital that is closed on that day, and this is ideal because it means that we don't disrupt the running of the building, or face interruptions from the public.

One of the main problems is that *Coronation Street* is such a high-profile programme, and the actors are immediately recognizable. Wherever we go we tend to attract a crowd, and although the artists are good about signing autographs, it is difficult for them to please their public and do their job at the same time. For this reason we try our best to protect the actors by finding self-contained locations where we can keep our presence quiet, but this does put parameters on where we can film. At locations where crowds are unavoidable, such as a day at a racecourse, we try to surround the actors with our own background artists, to prevent unsuspecting fans from dashing over when we are actually recording.

Further considerations to be taken into account are purely practical. Parking for the unit's trucks must be available close to the location but in a 'dead area' which will be out of shot of the camera. If we are using an electricity generator to power the equipment, it must be as close as possible to where we are filming, otherwise it becomes necessary to run cables to the location, which becomes a health and safety issue. Lighting and camera gear weighs a ton, so

Left: Director Michael Kerrigan and first assistant Dayle Evans.

that point and try to find the other locations close by so that we don't waste time on the day driving from one end of Manchester to the other.'

Domestic interiors can be tricky because the brief is so detailed that it is possible to go on looking for ever. One way to find the right place, though, is to locate a street which has the right style of housing, then drop letters through their doors, explaining that we are looking to film in the area and leaving a contact number for interested parties to ring. Generally speaking we meet with very little opposition from the residents, most of whom are only too delighted to have their homes appear on *Coronation Street*.

If we do decide to film in a residential area, Naomi arranges another letter drop to inform people that we are coming. No matter how professional the team, it is impossible to take a 40-

A busy
Monday.

wherever possible, we never go above the first floor of a building unless there is a lift big enough to accommodate it. As well as creating extra back-breaking work for the grips who have to carry the equipment, it is often necessary to light a set from outside through a window, which also becomes impossible if we go too high up. And filming too close to busy roads can be a nightmare because of the noise from the traffic.

Once all the criteria have been met, and Naomi has settled upon one location, it is necessary to do a technical recce. This takes place the Tuesday before filming begins and comprises the director, first assistant director, designer, camera crew leader, senior sound, lighting director and chief electrician. The director has already been on the initial recce and decided how to shoot the scenes; they will then talk the crew through the action so that everyone can work out what they will need on the day.

The chief electrician deduces what equipment to take, if they can use local power or whether to use the generator. The designer notes down any cosmetic changes to be made to the location and which props are needed. Sound, cameras and lighting make a note of any technical requirements, and the first assistant director books background artists, vehicles and specialist equipment like ladder pods or cranes. It is vital that everything is anticipated at this stage, as there is no time on a filming day to start running back to base for forgotten essentials.

After the technical recce is over, there is a lot of organizing to do over the next few days. The first will finalize the draft schedules, acting on the advice of the technical staff and director who may have a good practical reason for changing the shooting order after seeing the location. They will then note down the new call times and make sure everyone involved is aware of them.

From the point of view of the location manager, there are several logistical problems to be overcome before moving in with the cameras. Parking often involves getting permission from the police and the council, especially if filming is to take place in the city centre. Even on unrestricted roads the council are informed as a matter of courtesy, but often an area will be lined with parking meters, and Naomi has to get in touch with the Manchester Film Office to arrange for them to be bagged off overnight. Fortunately *Coronation Street* doesn't have separate make-up and wardrobe trucks and is quite a small, self-contained unit in comparison to other dramas.

Naomi books the caterers, and informs them how many people will be working and at what time to schedule the meal breaks. Breakfast is usually held at Granada Television, then they will drive to a unit base close to the location where they can park up and provide lunch. Again, a fee is paid to whoever owns the land.

Other facilities not booked by the technical staff include a small caravan for the artists to sit in when they are not on set, and mobile toilets if there are none available on site. There are limousines to be booked to collect the artists and minibuses for the extras, OSMs, make-up and wardrobe. Naomi books a security firm to look after the equipment during filming, and they also help park the unit up, often setting out first thing in the morning to cone off an area for the vehicles.

When the schedule is finalized, Naomi draws up a movement order to ensure that everybody knows where to go. This includes the name and address of the locations, a map and a set of written directions. It is also essential to have a working contact number for each location. If we are scheduled to begin filming at 7.00am we have to have somebody around to open up – and the worst thing that can happen is for the person with the keys to oversleep, especially if there is no way of getting hold of them!

On a typical day, Naomi will arrive at Granada in the morning and check that the caterers are up and running. Then she goes to meet the security men at the first location of the day and explain to them where everyone should be parked.

Generally the first assistant will drive the director and PA out in a car, and the rest of the crew go along in the minibus or in technical vehicles. Naomi or a unit manager stays around during filming to check that things are going smoothly, and keep an eye on the crew to make sure that no damage is done to the location. Any torn wallpaper or scratched paintwork is always made good afterwards by the unit's decorator, but generally speaking this problem doesn't arise.

'The crew are very experienced and are very careful with the equipment,' says Naomi. 'If they are filming in a room with a polished wooden floor they take boards to put down under the lamps so that it doesn't get scratched. And when we use someone's house, the set dresser always puts down dust sheets so that we don't ruin the carpets by traipsing in and out, especially on a wet day.'

By far and away the biggest problem on location, though, is one of noise. The *Coronation Street* studio is soundproofed, but in real locations we have no control over background noise. Central heating rumbles and clocks tick too loudly. Planes fly overhead, dogs bark, traffic goes past and burglar alarms are set off. All these things can delay filming, but unfortunately nothing can be done to prevent it. We are powerless over the weather. At the end of the day, if a scene needs completing we must film it whatever the conditions, and it is all too common an occurrence to have the wardrobe assistants hovering over artists with giant umbrellas to protect their clothing and make-up between takes. Occasionally, though, the

'I make sure they are happy with their scripts and prompt them if they forget their lines for a moment.'

weather can work in our favour. When Sharon Gaskell walked out of her own wedding ceremony and arrived back in *Coronation Street* in her dress to confront Natalie, there was a sudden snowstorm, which nobody could have planned for but which added considerably to the atmosphere of an already dramatic scene.

Sunday's location filming occurs off site, and filming on the lot usually takes place on Mondays. Granada Studio Tours jointly owns the set and it is necessary for the production team to liaise with them over use, as filming necessitates keeping the public away from this part of the tour. The outdoor set is not only used when characters are literally stood in the street. The sets for Underworld and Kevin's garage are also on the lot – and if there are more scenes than can reasonably be fitted in on one day we have to carefully negotiate with the tours to arrange extra filming time. It involves a certain amount of give and take, but satisfactory arrangements are always reached. Occasionally it will be necessary to barrier off the part of the set that is being used and let the public watch the filming. It isn't an ideal situation, but generally people are so delighted at being able to see *Coronation Street* in action that they don't disrupt the schedule and remain completely silent when the director calls for a take.

Unlike studio scenes, the location scenes are not camera scripted. The director can only decide which shots to take after he has been on a recce, seen the available space and noted down any restrictions, after which point the director and first assistant will get together to sort out all the nuts and bolts of the scene. Then, depending on how complicated it is going to be, the director might do a little thumbnail sketch for the producer's benefit.

In studio there are three cameras trained on the artists, each focusing on the action from a different point of view. On location there is only the one camera, but a single unwavering shot throughout a whole scene would be visually very dull for the viewer. Therefore, the scene has to be repeated again and again with the camera focusing on a different angle each time and then spliced together at the editing stage.

This can cause horrendous problems with continuity. The artists must remain in the same positions for each take or else the action will be impossible to pull together afterwards. The PA is the person responsible for continuity, and she has to be incredibly observant, writing down every tiny detail, no matter how insignificant it may seem.

'I make continuity notes before going out shooting, as well as during,' says PA Tina Kirk. 'If we've got a scene on the street set and there are three characters involved – say Gary, Jim and Kevin, then I'll look at the scene number and check where we last saw them. If we were shooting scene 5, and Gary had been seen leaving his house in scene 4, I would have to make sure that we film him coming out of his front door rather than walking down the street from a different direction. The director will often ask, "Have we seen Gary in the episode yet?" and because the scenes are shot out of sequence even the actors become confused. They will turn to me and say, "Where have I been?" and they also ask me about the

dialogue sometimes,' Tina adds. 'I make sure they are happy with their scripts and prompt them if they forget their lines for a moment. Some artists are better at remembering their lines than others and you have to know when to decide "That's about right", and go for the happy medium. As a PA you have to be able to get along with the artists at all times, and know when it is a good time to step in and give them prompts or continuity notes.'

The PA also has to make a minute study of each artist, because at any given point they could be asked whether an actress had their hair tucked behind their ear or hanging straight down, whether her hands were in her pockets or not, and which leg was crossed in front of the other a few moments ago. Despite the fact that most people would never have noticed such details in the first place, the PA will always be expected to know the answer.

'It's quite a hard thing to do – it's one of the most difficult parts of the job actually,' says Tina. 'I also mark up when they turn, when they move off, arrive or stop and what line they stop on, for each

Charge hand
Mick Horrocks
marks the
actors'
positions on
the floor.

take. If they walk out of frame I note down on which side, and I even look at which angle someone uses to pick up a glass or a mug.'

All location work is time-consuming, but certain scenarios are even more elaborate than normal and require painstaking and detailed planning. Events which take only a few seconds on screen can cause gargantuan amounts of work beforehand, even on a fast turnaround programme like *Coronation Street*, and viewers would be truly amazed if they realized how much work is frequently involved.

For example, scenes involving vehicles don't simply require an artist to get into a car and drive off. If we are to focus on them for any length of time, it becomes necessary to book a low loader – a lorry with a long low trailer upon which the car is positioned, surrounded by the crew. This means the crew can film through the windows of the car as the lorry moves, giving the impression of driving, but leaving the actors free to concentrate on their lines – and minimizing the risk of accidents. Sometimes it won't be feasible to arrange this in terms of time and a scene involving detailed car movements may have to be reworked. Even passing cars driving down *Coronation Street* are carefully choreographed, rather than random occurrences.

Charge hand Mick Horrocks marks the actors' positions on the floor.

One storyline a while ago involved Alma coming into some money and buying a sports car – the snag being that actress Amanda Barrie doesn't drive. Whenever we showed Mrs Baldwin at the wheel, a double of Amanda had to be found and the scene shot in two parts with a close-up of Amanda in the car and a long shot of her stand-in getting into gear and driving off.

Any scenes which may put an artist in danger will also mean using stunt doubles – and this can include something as simple as climbing down a ladder. Even if the artist is happy to perform the stunt themselves, we have to guarantee their safety and call stunt experts in to rig them up with concealed harnesses and wires – which sometimes means it is easier just to use a stunt person.

When special effects are called for, location filming becomes even more laborious. When Don Brennan was behaving irrationally a couple of years ago in the months running up to the demise of his character, his madness didn't only impact on the inhabitants of the street, but also on the production budget. In the space of a few weeks, Don set fire to Mike Baldwin's factory, drove Alma Baldwin into the docks, and then met a sticky end driving his car into the viaduct, whereupon the car burst into flames and he died in the wreckage.

The factory fire scenes involved huge amounts of work for both the design department and a team of special effects people. The aftermath of the inferno was filmed at a real factory, in front of which was built a façade based on photographs taken by the fire brigade. The construction was painted black and surrounded by various charred bits of debris, and a special effects expert added a trail of smoke made from charcoal and incense. An old roof set from a couple of years ago was retrieved, set on fire and than added to the top of the building, and the whole edifice was removed again once the brief scenes were shot.

The blaze was filmed at a safe building in the local fire brigade training centre, where a painstaking replica of Mike's stockroom was built, simply to be destroyed for the benefit of the cameras. A pyrotechnics team placed petrol bombs in strategic positions and

CORONATION STREET - Episodes 4632-4635

SHOOT WEEK 21

Production Office:	Tel: 0161 827 2538	Producer:	David Hanson
3rd Floor	Fax: 0161 827 2004	Production Executive:	Don Trafford 0831 25 44 12
GTV		Director:	Garth Tucker
		Location Manager:	Naomi Ellwood 0958 321 959
		OSM Desk:	Freddy-Carpen-Juckes 0161 832 7211
DATE:	Tuesday 25th May 1999	Production Co-ordinator:	Janette Munn 0411 862071/440 8074
UNIT CALL:	0730 – 1930		Police 0161 872 5050
M-UP/COS:			Hospital – Hope 0161 789 7373
			Alan Birch 07771 911 717
Sunrise/Set:	0455 – 2118		

PSC

Location 1	Int Pub	The Railway & Naturist Bury New Road Prestwich	Alan/Hazel 0161 773 9909
Location 2	Ext Park	Heaton Park Bury Old Road Prestwich Manchester	Jean 0161 773 1085
Location 3	Ext Coronation Street	The Lot	Naomi Ellwood 0958 321 959
Location 4	Int Underworld & Int Locker Room		

SC	PG	STORY TIME	SET	CHARACTERS
34/16	45-4	D3 1900	Int Pub	Steve, Lee, Elderly Customer
34/18	52-5	D3 1910	Int Pub	Steve, Lee
32/10	30-3	D1 1315	Ext Park	Rosie, Sally, Danny, Father
34/10	28	D3 1312	Ext Coronation Street	Mike, Roy, Linda
33/11	34-3	D2 1230	Ext Coronation Street	Jim, Ravi
33/8	24-2	D2 1100	Int Underworld Factory	Janice, Linda, Alison, Jean
34/2	4-7	D3 0905	Int Underworld Factory	Janice, Mike, Linda, Alison, Jean

MOVE TO STAGE ONE

SC	PG	STORY TIME	SET	CHARACTERS
33/5	14-1	D2 0904	Int Locker Room–Underworld	Janice, Linda, Alison, Jean
33/8pt	25	D2 1102	Int Locker Room–Underworld	Linda, Jean

CHARACTER	ARTISTE	COS/M'UP	READY
LEE SANKEY	STEPHEN GRAHAM	0700	0745
ELDERLY CUSTOMER	GERRY HINKS	0700	0745
STEVE MCDONALD	SIMON GREGSON	0730	0745
FATHER	ALAN PATTISON	0900	0945
SALLY WEBSTER	SALLY WHITTAKER	0900	0945
DANNY HARGREAVES	RICHARD STANDING	0915	0945
ROSIE WEBSTER	EMMA COLLINGE	0930	0945
MIKE BALDWIN	JOHNNY BRIGGS	1130	1215
ROY CROPPER	DAVID NEILSON	1145	1215
LINDA SYKES	JACQUELINE PIRIE	1145	1215
RAVI DESAI	SAEED JAFFREY	1215	1400
JEAN WALTERS	KATE LAYDEN	1230	1430
JIM MCDONALD	CHARLES LAWSON	1345	1400
JANICE BATTERSBY	VICKY ENTWISTLE	1345	1430
ALISON WAKEFIELD	NAOMI RADCLIFFE	1345	1430

These are your provisional call times. Please check with OSM on the evening before work to confirm that nothing has changed. Thank you.

DESCRIPTION:	EPISODE	CALL	COS/M'UP	TRAVEL	ON SET
NSES x 6	33,34	0700	-	0745	-
Street Regulars NSES x 7	32	0930	-	0945	-
Factory Girls x 3	33,34	1400	-	-	1430
Little Girl	32	0930	-	0945	-

DESIGN/PROPS:

NOTES:

BREAKFAST AT GTV FROM 0700

WOULD ALL ARTISTS PLEASE GO TO COSTUME BEFORE MAKE-UP

THANK YOU

DAYLE EVANS
FIRST ASSISTANT DIRECTOR

PSC call sheets.

laid further trails of petroleum around the set. Small fires were lit first, filmed and then put out and the scenes were cut together later. For the final explosion a backdraft was created with a compressed air cannon filled with fire gel which produced a fireball. Actor Geoff Hinsliffe used water instead of petrol to film Don's pyromaniac antics, then the special effects team set the real fire later on when the actor had been removed to safety. The camera was positioned in a special heat-resistant unit, sprinkler systems were rigged up and fire engines were on standby outside. The stunt cost thousands and took hours of work, yet was only seen for a matter of moments on screen.

Driving Alma into Weatherfield Quays was one of the most complicated stunts *Coronation Street* has ever attempted, and took five different 12-hour night shoots to complete, with both cast and crew working from 6.00am to 6.00pm. A suitable location had to be found and, as with any stunts involving water, professional divers were hired to trawl the depths to ensure there were no dangerous obstacles and support the stunt people who had to dive in. Next, a car had to have the oil, petrol and engine removed before being steam cleaned, so that the vehicle could be submerged in the water without causing a health hazard. The stunt car, complete with two plastic mannequins in the front seat dressed in identical clothes to actors Geoff Hinsliffe and Amanda Barrie, was attached to a tube connected to a compressed gas cylinder and then fired into the water.

Amanda's stunt double filmed the scenes where Alma swam free of the car, but the next night Amanda herself had to be submerged in freezing water for a close-up. As Amanda isn't trained in sub-aqua stunts, this was done at an entirely different, safer location – a tank of water at the fire brigade training centre with specially constructed ramps and platforms for Amanda to stand on.

Such Bond-like activities are by no means the norm in *Coronation Street*, and these stunts are relatively rare, but a great deal of the more everyday events also require detailed attention and meticulous planning. Viewers would be amazed if they could only see how much hard work and preparation goes into making their favourite programme, yet even when all the scenes are in the can, *Coronation Street* still has a long way to go before it is ready for transmission.

8
the
Putting

Programme

Together

Editing

By the time filming has finished on Friday evening, there are just over three weeks before the next block of four *Coronation Street* episodes are due to be transmitted. This means a race against time for the programme's editors.

Even on a show with such a tight shooting schedule, the director will end up with more material than is strictly necessary to tell the story. There will usually be several slightly different versions of each take, and it is the job of the editors to put together these disparate strands into the best possible finished version.

Coronation Street is edited on Avid, an off-line system that involves taking the completed tapes and feeding them into a digitiser that transforms the images into computer format. All the takes and scenes are stored on disc, and can be accessed separately.

This relatively new innovation has completely transformed the editing process. With on-line editing, decisions had to be made in linear order and if at the end of the process a director or editor changed their mind about the first few cuts, the whole rigmarole had to begin again from scratch.

With the off-line system, if they decide to amend a scene, wherever it occurs in the episode and at whatever stage in the

schedule, it is possible to make the alterations without affecting the rest of the footage. Any of the numbered shots can be instantly accessed and displayed, altered and changed back, ordered and re-ordered, saving an editor a huge amount of time and trouble as the programme can be modified literally at the touch of a button. The difference between Avid and the old, on-line system is rather like the difference between word processing and typing. If you decide to delete or swap paragraphs around on a word processor, it's a

Sophie Byrne in the editing suite.

simple process that doesn't affect the rest of the text, but on a manual typewriter the entire document would have to be re done.

As each scene can be dealt with as a separate entity, it enables us to turn round the tapes much more quickly. Because *Coronation Street* is shot out of sequence, the first scene of the first episode may only be recorded on Friday evening. If it were necessary to edit the scenes in story order this would only leave five days before the completed tape had to be ready. With the current system it is possible

to begin the editing process as soon as the first completed tapes arrive in the editing suites after PSC filming on the previous Sunday.

However, there are a couple of drawbacks. One is the time-consuming process of actually digitizing the tapes in the first place. It is a boring but necessary task that can't be shortened. Basically, if there are 20 hours of tape, they will take 20 hours to put into the machine.

Then, because the digitized pictures are not transmittable

quality, the entire four programmes have to be put back on to tape after the editing decisions have been made on computer. An edit decision list is taken down to the on-line suite and fed into their machines, and then the credits are added and the pictures colour corrected. After this point there would be major repercussions if any changes were to be made, so the version that goes to on-line is more or less the definitive one.

It is part of my job to view each episode before it is sent to on-line and add any changes of my own. But before the programmes are ready for my input, there is a lot of work to be done.

Whereas an episode will be virtually complete by the time I watch it, the editor has the tricky task of assembling it from scratch, which means making a lot of artistic decisions. Beginning on a Monday, the editor has a week (including the weekend) to work alone before getting feedback from the director and myself the next Monday. Often this involves working until midnight if there are a lot of long, busy scenes, and the Avid machines, like any computer, may go down from time to time to further confound matters. But while the technical demands of editing may look complicated to the average person, the most difficult part of the job is not accumulating the computer know-how, but deciding when and where to cut a scene to deliver the maximum impact, while progressing the story in a seamless way.

The editing suites for *Coronation Street* are situated next to each other, separated by a small room that houses the machinery for digitising the tapes. Each suite contains two ordinary-looking large-screen computers with multicoloured keyboards, which are linked up so that images can be moved from one to the other, and it is here that the editor, and later the director, sit for hours on end perfecting the final programme.

'The best editing is where the viewer doesn't notice it's been done,' says Sophie Byrne, who along with Pete Deacon is one of the two off-line editors who work alternately on blocks of four episodes. 'You have to show the audience what they want to see, when they want to see it, but they shouldn't actually notice where you cut from one shot to another. It's not an exact science, though. It's all opinion and choice, and another thing is that a programme is never really finished – it's just abandoned. You can always keep on editing and re-editing for ever, but at some point you have to decide when to stop.'

There is a difference between editing scenes shot in studio and material done on location. PSC scenes come in first because they are shot at the beginning of the week, and just as they take longer to record, being on a single camera, so they also take longer to edit.

Studio scenes have already been vision mixed, and if this has worked as expected they are almost the finished article when they arrive in the editing suite – although there are also separate tapes from each camera which have been shot all the way through to give

'The best editing is where the viewer doesn't notice it's been done . . . You have to show the audience what they want to see, when they want to see it, but they shouldn't actually notice where you cut from one shot to another.'

where it begins and ends. To the uninitiated a marked-up script would look indecipherable, but it is invaluable to an editor.

'It can look a bit baffling, but it's just shorthand, nothing technical,' assures Sophie. 'MCU stands for medium close-up, ISO means an isolated shot, 2S stands for two-shot (meaning two characters are in the frame) and so on. The PA will also have written little notes such as "end on Fred" or "hold on Jack" and filled in any slight script changes.'

Sometimes, although three or four takes will have been filmed, the director may already have decided that the first few didn't work, and so the PA will have indicated which one the editor should use. In this case, the duff takes won't even be digitized and the editor will just have the approved ones to work with. There may also be pick-ups, shots which just comprise a small part of a scene – for example, if an actor fluffs one line but the rest of the scene is fine, just that part will be redone, and again this is indicated on the script.

One of the most onerous and time-consuming tasks is ensuring each programme is the correct running time. When each scene has been edited and put together in story order, the editor must take the timings and begin trimming or stretching the episodes to exactly 24 minutes. Every second counts and an editor will go through the scenes one by one, taking off a fraction of a second here and there until the episode is the required length. Sometimes

the editor and director more flexibility. The director has thought about the final shots even before going into studio, and the continuity is already in place, because the three cameras have been recording simultaneously.

PSC material consists of several shots, taken from different angles, which need painstakingly putting together, and can give rise to a number of problems. It is at this point that an editor really appreciates having had an efficient PA/script supervisor the week before, because their script notes are one of the keys to the editing process.

An editor will use the scripts as a starting point. Unlike studio scenes, those filmed on PSC aren't camera scripted, so the PA will have filled in what has been shot. From this, an editor can see which tape a scene is on and what happens in it. The master tape and guard (back-up) tape numbers and scene running times are given, and each numbered take is marked down with a timecode, briefly described and a line drawn alongside the dialogue to show

a whole scene can be lost and dialogue can also be removed, as long as the omission isn't detrimental to the continuity and quality of the overall programme.

The director goes into the edit suite the following Monday, and the process of fine cuts begins. This is the perfecting of the finished product and is a very intricate process. There are 25 frames a second on screen, and sometimes removing even a couple of these frames can make the difference between a good scene and an indifferent one.

It is very beneficial at this stage to have another person's input, because an editor will have been working on the programme so closely over the past few days that it is possible to miss things. The director will look at the overall rhythm of the programme and remove anything that is visually jarring. They may also change a few angles, or pick up on a continuity problem that has been missed. Or they may ask for some extra wild tracks – re-recorded sound which can be added on, which an artist will come in and do in the audio dubbing suite later in the week.

The Cadbury's sponsorship messages are added on before and after the programme and before and after the advertisement break. These are scheduled beforehand by Cadbury's, and the editors work from a list to see which promotional film to show on which date. Then the end shot for the credits is added. For years the only available shot to screen the credits over was one of the famous rooftops, but these days we occasionally see a darker shot of the cobbles at night. If there is a particularly dramatic episode, some footage may be shot separately and the credits can roll over the final frames of the last scene, but the tiled roofs and chimney pots remain *Coronation Street*'s most enduring image in the minds of the public.

I view the programme at this stage and add any changes of my own. I often work from home on a Monday as I have a lot of reading to do, and the first tape will arrive at my house by courier on Monday afternoon. I watch it straight away and phone the editor and director with my amendments. The second tape arrives later that evening or early Tuesday morning, and by Wednesday I will have viewed all four episodes and given my final approval.

While the editor and director will have already selected the best takes for performances and technical values, examined the continuity and ensured the finished product is the right length, as producer I look at the finished episodes from another perspective. As well as being satisfied that each episode is of a suitably high quality, and is as absorbing and emotionally resonant as possible, I look for things like compliance problems – for example, too much accidental emphasis on brand-name consumer goods, which is against the ITC's strict restrictions on product placement. I also check for story issues. Sometimes a director or editor may have cut a scene in order to trim the time, not realising its importance to the overall plot, so I may ask for it to be reinstated and suggest other cuts. I will rarely unpick much material, and any changes I make at this stage will have a valid artistic or practical reason behind them.

Although the programme is virtually complete by now, watching it is an odd experience. At first you don't realise what is wrong, and then it hits you – there are no background noises. The Rovers regulars in the background are mouthing words but nothing comes out. The jukebox is never on in the cafe. Doors slam, but almost silently. And there are no traffic noises, no sewing machines buzzing in the factory, and no radio in the garage.

This is because *Coronation Street* likes to record 'clean' sound, which means recording the dialogue but keeping it as free as possible from background effects. This makes it easier to edit. For example, if we were filming Les and Janice talking in the street, there may be several takes – first with the camera on Les, then with the camera on Janice, then with a two-shot, and at varying degrees of close-up. These different takes would be spliced together at the editing stage, but if a plane were flying overhead on the first take but not the second the sound would be discontinuous as the point of view switched from Les to Janice and back again. Some noise can be removed later, but it is difficult if it coincides with the character speaking. And if the dubbing editor had to spend hours picking out bits of background noise, we would never be able to produce four episodes each week. Therefore at this stage the only sound on the tapes tends to be the principal artists' dialogue.

Then, after going to a great deal of trouble to keep the takes free of background noise, it has to be painstakingly put back on again. It takes three long days in the audio dubbing suite to do this, but years and years of experience have proved this to be the best method. The most real-sounding noise is actually faked!

The episodes go to be dubbed as soon as they have been finished in off-line. It takes between four and six hours to dub each 24-minute episode. Just as the editors' computers allow them to cut and paste pictures like a word processor cuts and pastes text, so an audio file allows the dubbing editor to cut and paste pieces of sound into the programme. The sound is separate from the pictures at this point, so the dubbing editor joins them together again, resyncs the sound with the pictures and evens over the edits where there have been any jumps or changes in atmosphere, before adding the background noises.

The director tells the dubbing editor which specific effects are wanted, and where. Some directors like to have music in the Rovers, some don't. Occasionally they may suggest a particular style or piece of music – perhaps classical or light jazz in a restaurant, something smoochy for a romantic scene in somebody's flat, or a popular local radio station in the hair salon. The choice of music is limited by what the music department can clear, and each week they send down whichever chart songs are currently available.

Next the sound is split across 16 tracks. Four of these are sync sound, which has been recorded on location or in studio, and the other 12 are for additional effects, such as traffic noise. There are thousands and thousands of effects available – up to ten hours' worth of assorted sound, all stored in an audio file. There are dogs barking, cars passing, doors slamming, washing machines whirring

'We get people writing in saying they heard a bird song in the background and that particular bird isn't heard in northern Britain at that time of year.'

and doorbells ringing, and choosing the right sound requires a real ear for detail.

'There are techniques, but it's trial and error really, and a case of trusting your own ears,' says dubbing editor Martin Whitley. 'You have to judge what sounds right, and it helps if you are quite observant. If you are in a pub, does it have a restaurant? Would you hear pots and pans and people eating? What style of pub is it? What type of music would they play? How many people are in there? It's no good putting on a chat track of 400 people in a village hall when there are only about ten people in the scene you are working with, so you have to gauge the right level of sound.'

For background conversation we have a stock library of fairly anonymous noise. There is a stereo track and a mono track and the two are mixed and matched to give the effect of randomness and avoid repetition. Sometimes we record our own background noise if there is something specific, but instead of recording it at the same time as the main dialogue of the scene, it is taped separately afterwards. If Deirdre were talking to Mike in Underworld and the factory girls were laughing and joking in the background, Deirdre and Mike's dialogue would be recorded first with the girls miming a raucous din in the background, and then a 'wild track' would be made of the machinists' revelries.

Some effects are already in place – the beer pumps in the Rovers

actually work, so there is no need to add on the sound of pints being poured. The door, however, is silent because it is on the studio set, so every time we see the Rovers door close, the 'thump' as it swings shut has been added on. We also have sound effects for the shop tills because they are generally switched off. And when a character comes downstairs, we add their footsteps, as in reality none of the sets' stairs go all the way to the top – and in some cases there are no stairs at all, and the artist will simply be stood outside the set awaiting their cue.

'There are also times when the real effect you have recorded doesn't sound right, so we replace it with a better version,' adds Martin. 'If you record someone knocking on a door from the perspective of where they are standing it doesn't sound right at all, so we replace it with door knocks recorded at a greater distance, which is how people imagine them to sound.'

As with editing, the best dubbing is when you don't notice it is there. The effect we are striving for is one of real life – and if we get it wrong, it's amazing how observant viewers spot the mistakes.

'We get people writing in saying they heard a bird song in the background and that particular bird isn't heard in northern Britain at that time of year,' says Martin. 'We also get criticized if a diesel car goes by and we put a petrol engine noise on it, or a motorbike whizzes past sounding like a moped, so we have to be very careful.'

As the sound is being completed, the programme is simultaneously being transferred to an on-line version suitable for transmission, and it is at this point that the credits, which have

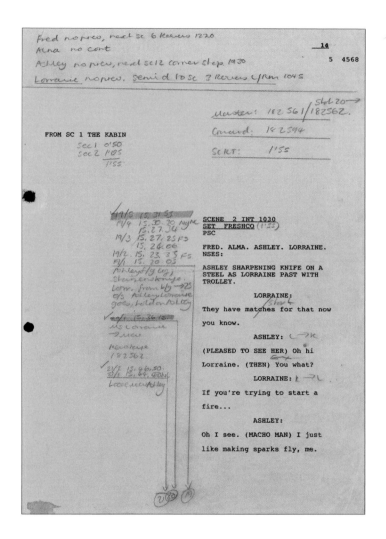

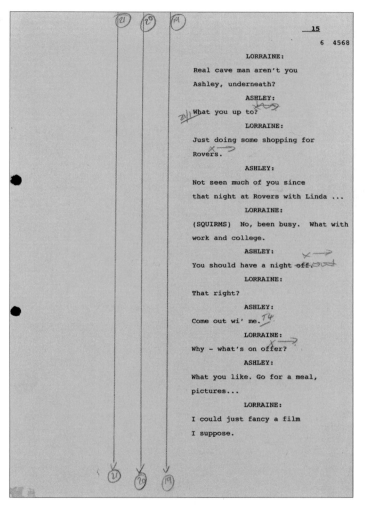

Camera scripts used by the editors.

been compiled by the PA, are added over the final shot. Then the tapes are ready for transmission.

When the editing has been completed, the PA will watch VHS tapes of the final cut and make up a script from this version which is sent to the ITFC for subtitling. The production assistant also arranges for everything to be technically previewed and the tapes to be made and sent off, and on the following Monday compiles PIPs or Programme Information Packs. These consist of paperwork for the ITV Network Centre including synopses of the programme, and details of the final running times.

The PA also makes up the *Coronation Street* omnibus which is shown in the Granada region, amalgamating the Wednesday and Friday episodes from the block and trimming it by a minute to cut the total running time to 46 minutes and 30 seconds.

Finally, all the information pertaining to the episodes is put into a programme file that is kept in the archive department. It is now only days until the episodes are scheduled to be shown on television – and once the programme has been screened there is still further work to be done, dealing with the reaction from both the press and the public.

9

Beyond
the
Small
Screen

Coronation Street Press and Publicity

With around 18 million viewers per episode, and a permanent position at the top of the UK's ratings, *Coronation Street* is a media phenomenon. Today more than ever, the programme has become a multi-million-pound industry, rarely out of the public eye.

The outdoor set doubles up as a tourist attraction; a long list of licensees produce a wide range of *Coronation Street*-related merchandise under the umbrella of Granada Media Consumer Products, and we have a record-breaking sponsorship deal with Cadbury's chocolate. The *Street* has a fan club, and also maintains a comprehensive Internet site which provides information, interviews and chat rooms for a huge army of fans from all over the world. Both this and the many unofficial sites carry updates of episodes being screened in every country, and the show's many enthusiasts correspond with each other on a daily basis about the characters and plots.

The *Street* is even becoming a widespread academic subject. We have an education pack available for schoolchildren doing projects on the programme, and university students are increasingly beginning to study *Coronation Street* as a cultural text on several media studies courses.

The monumental fascination with *Coronation Street* is not lost on the media. Such is its popularity that newspapers, magazines and television and radio shows are all eager to feature the *Street* and capitalize on the programme's marketability. And with such intense scrutiny from both the press and the viewing public, it is essential

The press turn out en-masse for a photocall.

The public enjoy Coronation Street.

that we have the resources to manage the overwhelming interest. To this end, there are several different departments working at full tilt to respond to the world's obsession with *Corrie.*

The *Street's* press officers have the demanding job of co-ordinating the vast amount of programme publicity. Given the amount of interest already present, publicizing the *Street* might seem like a dream occupation, with no hard sell necessary in order to get the programme in the papers. But the show's high profile brings its own problems and dilemmas.

Most television dramas have a beginning, a middle and an end, and a publicist can decide exactly how to promote it and which publications to pitch it at, and are able to formulate a strategy accordingly. By comparison, *Coronation Street* is like a runaway train. Although tactics are planned and followed through with

regard to certain storylines, it is much harder to maintain control over the public image of a programme that is screened four nights a week, 52 weeks a year, particularly as everybody wants a piece of it. Rather than being as pro-active as they would like to be, press officers Alison Sinclair and Janice Troup, and assistants Iain Hoskins and Stuart King, spend a lot of their time simply reacting to the huge volume of requests. Many of the problems and queries that they are called upon to deal with aren't always strictly programme related.

'A large part of the job is firefighting,' explains Alison Sinclair. 'Some people would argue that it is easy to publicize *Coronation Street* because everybody is interested in it and you are guaranteed coverage. But the hard part is trying to ensure that it is the publicity you want rather than the publicity the press sometimes want to give you.'

'Some people would argue that it is easy to publicize *Coronation Street* because everybody is interested in it and you are guaranteed coverage. But the hard part is trying to ensure that it is the publicity you want rather than the publicity the press sometimes want to give you.'

Hundreds of column inches are devoted to the programme each week, and every small detail becomes news. When Reg Holdsworth moved to Lowestoft, we were immediately besieged by calls from the Lowestoft area asking why we chose their town. Also, prior to that, we ran a story about Reg's waterbed bursting during a passionate exchange with Maureen Naylor. This prompted several anxious bedroom furnishing companies to telephone the newspapers assuring them this was a rare occurrence, and that waterbeds weren't prone to self-destruction, no matter what people had seen on the *Street*.

Because of *Coronation Street*'s astonishingly high profile, every aspect of the programme is subject to investigation. The folk of Weatherfield are so familiar to the British people that they are even used in newspapers' financial sections to illustrate matters such as how the budget would affect a 'typical' low-income family like the Mallets or a small businessman like Mike Baldwin.

As well as this, individual storylines must be publicized in order to maximize the viewing figures. Press releases giving a taster of what is to happen in the show are sent out a couple of weeks beforehand, as are preview VHS tapes. Stills photographer Neil

Marland is despatched to take pictures of the key dramatic or funny scenes as they are filmed each week, and these are made freely available to the press. Listings and women's magazines are made aware of the upcoming storylines so they can plan their schedule of covers and interviews, and the cast participate in special photo sessions and interviews to assuage the insatiable demand for information. However, many viewers find it infuriating when they discover the dénouement of a plot too soon, and the press office strive to achieve a careful compromise between satisfying curiosity and spoiling the suspense.

'You have to balance it because publicity for a programme is all about getting people to tune in,' explains Janice Troup. 'Most people who are regular viewers will watch the show anyway, but there are others who dip in and out of the programme. The argument is that if they have drifted away, and then they read about something that is about to happen which intrigues them, they will start watching again. It has been proved that you can add up to three million viewers with a really strong piece of publicity in a high-selling tabloid newspaper on the day of publication, coupled with TV listings magazine covers.'

A cover
shoot takes
place.

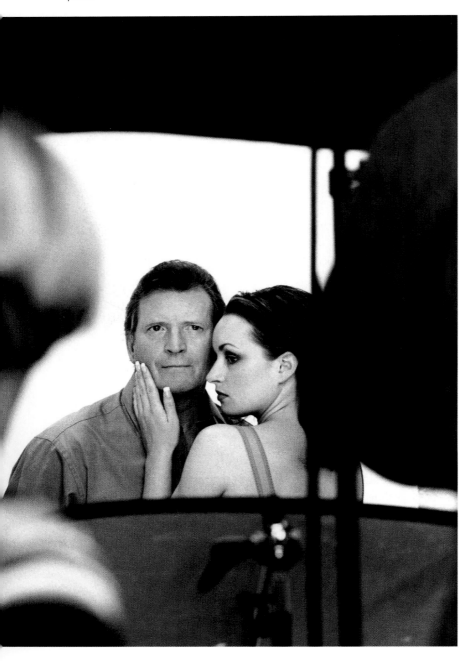

However, that isn't to say that it is not frustrating when a newspaper chooses to blow a storyline three months in advance for no other reason than to boost its own circulation. The difference is that when Granada release information in a controlled way, the story has already gone so far that the advance details don't ruin the enjoyment of what goes before. When a tabloid leaked the news that Leanne was to have an abortion several weeks before it was due to happen, it simply caused frustration for everyone concerned because it negated the build-up of her being pregnant. Such leaks are infuriating, but however careful we are to maintain confidentiality, sometimes – unavoidably – storylines slip through the net.

The storylines aren't the only thing to interest the media, though. These days, with the culture of celebrity stronger than ever, many viewers know almost as much about the artists portraying the *Street* characters as they do about the fictional families whose lives they follow on screen. Several years ago, a cartoon from a well-known daily newspaper depicted the cast of *Coronation Street* gathered around the Rovers Return bar, where the director was announcing through a megaphone, 'Throw your scripts away, and just carry on talking about your private lives.' The cartoon hung in the Green Room for many years but, although it is now no longer on the wall, the cast hardly need reminding of their fame. Artists are inundated with personal interview requests, photographed at awards ceremonies and even snapped walking to the shops by keen paparazzi who know that their every action is of interest to the viewing public.

Nothing is beneath the attention of the press when it comes to *Corrie*. Most special-interest magazines are desperate to know if there are any *Street* stars that share their readers' enthusiasms. Vegetarian magazines phone wanting to know which cast members are veggies and what their favourite recipes are. Holiday supplements call to find out their favourite destinations. Animal lovers' magazines ring up wanting to know what type of pets they have, and handicraft publications are curious to know if anyone

from the cast does tapestry in their spare time.

Tabloids also treasure the trivia. If they think they've spotted an actor sporting a tattoo or a new hairstyle, they'll want to know all about it. The press office once fielded a call from the *Mirror* who wanted to know if an elderly actress was wearing a new hearing aid or not. Christmas brings forth queries concerning what the cast would most like to find in their stockings, and at New Year everyone is keen to hear their resolutions.

National events are rarely allowed to pass without some sort of *Street* input. Whenever there is a debate about licensing laws, there are invariably journalists who want to know the opinions of the actor or actress currently playing the landlord or lady of the Rovers Return. The fact they are talking to performers rather than publicans, who probably have little or no interest in the subject, often seems to get overlooked. Important sporting events bring queries about which stars are rooting for which team, and during the last World Cup, the

newspapers were delighted when some of the ladies from the cast agreed to don the strips of their favourite players.

Many of the calls are lighthearted. Cliff Richard's office once called the *Street* publicists to ask if they could send him some videotapes as he'd been away and missed a few episodes. And when Julie Goodyear left, the two leading tabloid newspapers fell over themselves to secure the last pair of earrings she wore on screen for a readers' competition. When the *Sun* journalist called with his request and was told the baubles had already been promised to the *Mirror*, he even asked if it would be possible to split the pair so that the two rivals could have an earring each.

One of the most spectacular press triumphs in the show's history was the incredible coverage of the Free Deirdre Rachid campaign. As a treasured character of 25 years standing, we expected the storyline where the gullible widow was duped into an affair with conman Jon Lindsay to cause some concern amongst

'I received a call on 1 April from Tony Blair's office asking if we could update them on the situation, and I seriously thought it was an April Fool so I asked them to give me their name and number so I could call them back.'

viewers. But we were astounded by their reaction when, on 29 March 1998, she was sentenced to 18 months' imprisonment in front of over 20 million viewers.

On screen, the residents of Weatherfield, led by Mike, Ken and Emily, campaigned vigorously for her release. But off screen, the cries of 'Free The Weatherfield One' rang even louder. National newspapers took the story to heart, calling the court case 'Television's Trial of the Century', and acres of newsprint were devoted to Deirdre's dilemma. On the night that Deirdre was pronounced guilty, hordes of tearful fans called Granada Television's duty officer to protest her innocence, and the phones were busy for hours.

The *Sun* and the *Star* began selling Free Deirdre T-shirts and window stickers, and across the country petitions were signed and demonstrations staged. Workers at a foundry in South Wales downed tools for an hour to protest at her sentence; an escapologist from Sussex offered his services to help her break out; and a Kent pub landlord changed the name of his hostelry from Thompson's

Bell to Free Deirdre until her release. Even notorious villains such as Ronnie Knight and Frankie Fraser spoke to newspapers about the miscarriage of justice in *Coronation Street*.

Fiction blurred into fact still further as the Free Deirdre campaign was reported on the national television news. Tony Blair was drawn into the debate after Labour MP Fraser Kemp brought up the subject during Prime Minister's Question Time, and demanded that Home Secretary Jack Straw intervene.

'I received a call on 1 April from Tony Blair's office asking if we could update them on the situation, and I seriously thought it was an April Fool so I asked them to give me their name and number so I could call them back,' laughs Alison Sinclair. 'I really thought I was going to be on a wind-up on a radio station, but it turned out to be genuine.'

However, the hype was enormously beneficial. 'It was actually worked out that if we had paid in advertising for the amount of column inches we commanded, it would have cost Granada £1.5 million to do the campaign,' Alison reveals. 'It was bigger than any

of us could have imagined, and I think that people genuinely believed that they had some say in her being released when she was set free. They felt they had played a part in *Coronation Street* history and in storylines being made.'

However, not all press attention is so benevolent, and there is also a huge appetite for salacious gossip and intimate details of the actors' private lives. Whenever a new member of cast joins the programme it is made clear to them that their lives will never be the same. They are also warned of the fact that anything in their background may well be rooted out by the papers, whether or not they wish to guard their privacy. But it is hard to prepare someone for the sheer volume of attention they are invariably going to be subjected to – some of it very unpleasant.

'The hardest part of this job is the crisis management, and that is one of the things that makes it stand out from any other programme,' confirms Janice. 'We try to protect the artists' personal lives, but there will always be those phone calls that come in at 6.00 on a Friday night when you least expect them. We ask the cast to tell us if anything happens to them, and to let us know if they have been photographed or approached by the press. We try to remain one step ahead, but often we have to deal with something that is really upsetting for the cast member it has happened to. If their personal lives are then splashed all over the papers it is really going to impact on them.'

But whilst the press can be foe, they also have another, friendlier face. The glamorous side of the *Street* sees the actors and actresses being invited to take luxury holidays in exotic locations, which are then featured in glossy magazines. Top stylists and photographers are keen to take their pictures, and there is also the whirl of showbusiness openings, premières and awards to attend – for which top designers are often more than happy to let actors borrow their clothes.

One of the highlights of the *Coronation Street* year is the anniversary party which is held as close as possible to 9 December, the date the first ever episode was screened, and therefore marks the start of the Christmas party season. This glittering occasion is

always fully attended by the cast, their partners, crew members and television executives, and each year a photograph of the actors in their glamorous evening clothes is distributed to the press.

Daran Little makes the arrangements for the cast to attend the big industry ceremonies such as the BAFTAs and the National Television Awards. At this year's Soap Awards *Coronation Street* won the overall award for Best Soap. Individual accolades went to Stephen Billington (Villain of the Year), John Savident (Best Comedy Performance), David Neilson and Julie Hesmondhalgh (Best Partnership) and Bill Roache (Special Achievement Award). Daran's office, which is responsible for all archive material, is also involved at another level – choosing the clips to be shown as the nominees are read out.

Every *Coronation Street* episode ever made is still in existence, and copies reside in the tape library at Yorkshire Television. The contents of each video have been meticulously detailed and entered into the computer system by Daran, who watched 14 episodes a day for three years to complete the task, and who still ensures the

files are updated regularly from the scripts.

For awards ceremonies, clips are chosen to demonstrate the merit of the actor nominated for an award – dramatic, emotional or funny examples of their performances. If an artist is to be a guest on a chat show the researchers often ask for something to illustrate their current storylines and occasionally programmes wanting to highlight a particular issue request more specific extracts from the show. As a rule, we don't release material just to illustrate points, but each case is individual and all clips are authorized by Daran or myself. Then once they have been sourced, a transfer is organized and extract sales are notified to deal with search and handling fees and artists' royalties.

Thanks to the carefully cross-referenced database, each character's life history from the day they first appeared in the *Street* is available at the touch of a button. The comprehensive character information also includes supplementary details such as their date of birth, parents' names and occupations and previous marital and career histories – even prior to their introduction into the programme.

'The power of this programme is that whatever issue *Coronation Street* mentions, we will receive a call from a publication that deals with that area.'

As well as facilitating the otherwise long-winded task of finding clips, the database assists Daran in ironing out any glitches in the scripts or storylines, and means that he can answer literally any question about *Coronation Street* that a magazine, newspaper, fan or researcher could possibly ask. Having worked on the programme since 1989, and as a long-term fan who wrote his degree dissertation on Tony Warren's original characters, he has also committed an enormous amount of information to memory. Daran can usually answer the most obscure queries without hesitation, and is in demand as a guest on radio and television programmes whenever the *Street* is one of the subjects under discussion.

Whilst it is important for continuity that the characters' personal details are correct right down to their wedding anniversaries, it is also vital that we don't slip up when it comes to real life. Arbitrary things that don't ring true have a jarring effect on the audience, and although *Coronation Street* is fiction, the framework has to be rooted in genuine fact.

For this reason, we have to thoroughly research every storyline

we cover – a job which also falls to Daran's office, although the writers often do a lot of their own research too. When Jackie Dobbs was squatting in Curly Watts' house, we had to be aware of both his and her legal rights. When Jim was awarded disability benefit after his accident, we needed to know exactly how much money he was entitled to. The medical details of Jack's angina were carefully researched, and when Roman remains were discovered on the Red Rec, signalling victory for Spider's campaign against the Millennium Bowl, our researcher at the time had to get in touch with the British Museum. We asked them to fax an illustration of a stridgel, or bath tool, so the design department could make a convincing copy of one.

'The power of this programme is that whatever issue *Coronation Street* mentions, we will receive a call from a publication that deals with that area,' says Alison. 'If there's a nursing story, *Nursing Times* call, if there's a story involving a pond, we'll get pond keepers' magazines on the line and so on.'

Because of this, and because of the constant volume of letters from the public, we must pay attention to detail. Years ago, we received a barrage of complaints from ornithologically minded viewers when we mixed up Mavis and Percy's budgies and the female budgie Harriet was seen on screen playing male bird Randy. Apparently in close-up a mark on the beak gave away our mistake, and ruined the episode for several twitchers.

Daran Little in his office.

As well as advice and opinions, we also receive a daily dose of complaints, compliments and questions from fans around the world. Enthusiasts of all ages and nationalities keep in touch via phone, fax, letters and e-mail. Queries and comments are regularly sent to the *Coronation Street* website and e-mail address. Reams of letters are fielded by the *Coronation Street* production office, and many more are dealt with via the duty office, whose job it is to listen to viewers' enquiries at all hours of the day and night.

Compliments and complaints all have to be logged, and if there are more than ten complaints over the same thing we pass them on to the ITC who will adjudicate on the matter. As producer, I make a point of seeing any strong views that are expressed and do my best to answer as many letters as possible.

Coronation Street is often targeted by well-meaning groups wanting to put their views across, as the programme is rightly seen as having a far-reaching influence, but it simply isn't possible to incorporate all perspectives. Of course the creative team try to act responsibly when deciding upon storylines, but it isn't up to the *Street* to preach to audiences.

Anti-smoking lobbyists call to complain about cigarette consumption in the show, and Leanne's abortion provoked dismay amongst pro-life campaigners even though the issue was treated sensitively and the termination was shown to be a difficult and traumatic decision for the teenager. However, *Coronation Street* is first and foremost a drama serial, and whilst we acknowledge our responsibility to the viewer and carefully consider the implications of storylines, it is impossible to please absolutely everybody.

Over the last 18 months there have been almost 7000 calls registered either complaining about issues on *Coronation Street* or congratulating us on our handling of them, but these are just the tip of the iceberg as we receive many more from people simply requiring general information.

'I try to take away as many calls as possible from the production department, because otherwise they wouldn't have time to make the programme,' says duty officer David Nugent. 'I send out up to 40 sets of signed pictures every single day – our budget for cast photographs alone is £7000 per quarter. I also send out souvenirs from the show for charity auctions and answer general questions. On an average day I answer about 30 phone calls, 30 letters and several e-mails, but sometimes there can be many more. People feel very strongly about *Coronation Street*. For a lot of our viewers it really is part of their lives and they won't miss it for anything.'

Many of the calls are amusing. When Les Battersby had a van for sale, we received three calls offering to buy it within five minutes of the programme being screened. Offers come in for houses on the street, and we receive cards for characters getting married and wreaths for those who die. One viewer sent a cheque for £5000 for the Free Deirdre fund – which of course was

promptly returned. But it is incredible just how much the viewers identify with *Coronation Street* and it indicates how the programme has permeated the national consciousness.

When *Coronation Street* was first broadcast in 1960, television was still in its infancy, with very few programmes and channels to choose from. Now, with satellite and cable television, the digital revolution well underway, and hundreds of new channels available, programme makers have to struggle to hold an audience's attention.

As home entertainment proliferates, there is a danger that one day nobody will have any viewing habits in common. Yet *Coronation Street* has gone from strength to strength over the years, changing and adapting to match its audience whilst still encompassing the traditional values that people expect from the show. I fully believe that the *Street* will continue to grow in popularity well into the millennium, and retain its loyal army of fans right into its fortieth year and beyond.

Having had a hugely enjoyable and successful year in charge of the main programme, I will next be taking over the post of Producer - *Coronation Street* Special Projects which will help steer the show well into the celebrations of its fortieth year. *Coronation Street's* massive popularity and increasing success means that there will be more interest than ever leading up to this special birthday and as the show goes from strength to strength its many fans can rest assured that everyone concerned will ensure it remains where it belongs . . . at the top. Here's to the next forty years!

David Hanson, August 1999